THE REQUIREMENTS OF DEMOCRATIC FOREIGN POLICY

PACEM IN TERRIS III

Volume I
The Nixon-Kissinger Foreign Policy:
Opportunities and Contradictions

Volume II
The Military Dimensions
of Foreign Policy

Volume III
American Foreign Policy in the
Age of Interdependence

Volume IV
The Requirements of
Democratic Foreign Policy

The Requirements of Democratic Foreign Policy

Congress, the President, Partisanship,
the Foreign Policy Establishment
and the Media

Edited by
Fred Warner Neal and Mary Kersey Harvey

Volume IV of four volumes edited from the proceedings of
PACEM IN TERRIS III
A National Convocation to Consider
New Opportunities for United States Foreign Policy,
Convened in Washington, D.C., October 8-11, 1973, by
the Center for the Study of Democratic Institutions

49991

Center for the Study of Democratic Institutions
2056 Eucalyptus Hill Road
Santa Barbara, California 93108

Library of Congress Catalog Card Number: 74-78885
ISBN Cloth Set 0-87182-100-1
ISBN Cloth Vol. IV 0-87182-104-4
ISBN Paper Set 0-87182-105-2
ISBN Paper Vol. IV 0-87182-109-5

Designed by Barbara Monahan.
Printed in the United States of America.

Acknowledgments

The Center for the Study of Democratic Institutions gratefully acknowledges financial support for *Pacem in Terris III* from the Businessmen's Education Fund, and from the more than 4,000 Center members who sent special donations or attended the Washington sessions. Dissemination of the proceedings through television broadcast was made possible by grants from the IBM Corporation to the National Production Center for Television, and from the Frances Drown Foundation to the Center.

Harry S. Ashmore
President

Contents

Introduction

It is appropriate that the fourth and last volume of the *Pacem in Terris III* series on foreign policy should deal with the requirements of democratic foreign policy. In terms of the process by which such policy is formulated, the United States faces not only a need for new directions in its dealings with a rapidly changing world, but profound challenges to the means by which we have arranged and carried out our international relations. In a democracy, the process of government is as important as the substance of its acts; abuse of one leads to corruption of the other. For at least a decade the American people have displayed a spreading awareness that something has gone wrong in Washington, and these doubts and fears were rooted initially in public reaction to the Cold War policies that had their climax in the debacle in Indochina. What began with a widening credibility gap in the Johnson Administration became a constitutional crisis in the second term of President Nixon.

Beyond the personalities and partisanship engendered by the Watergate revelations, the central issues turn on the proper limits of executive authority—not merely the powers of the President himself, but those lodged in the gargantuan executive establishment which began its mushroom growth on the eve of World War II and has continued to expand ever since. The areas seen by many to be beyond the presumed center of our governmental system of checks and balances are those concerned with foreign policy and military policy.

Despite all the considerable efforts of the framers of the Constitution to limit executive power, its growth is perhaps the single most significant feature in the modern development of the federal government. Although a few constitutional experts always found the pattern worrisome, prior to World War II political leaders did not regard the occasional emergence of a "strong president" as particularly serious. Exceptional power assumed by the executive to deal with crises lapsed after the crises were over, and the country each time returned to the more or less even constitutional tenor of its ways. Moreover, through most of the history of the United States, the special executive prerogatives in the conduct of foreign policy were of little concern because to an inward-looking nation international relations were only a minor concern. The lack of constitutional precision about the extent of presidential authority in this area sometimes produced disputes, but they were not critical.

After World War II the situation suddenly was different. The war-time powers of the presidency—greatly enlarged over anything known before by the nature of the global conflict—continued into peacetime. The justification was the Cold War, in which the national security of the United States was held to be in continuing jeopardy. "Emergency" followed "emergency." With American armed forces already spread around the globe, the Congressional power to declare war was eclipsed. And with the rise of institutions like the Central Intelligence Agency, a shield of official secrecy was erected against the traditional oversight of Congress, and the inquiries of the press.

There was, it should be said on behalf of the Cold War presidents, no conscious intention to distort the traditional constitutional balance, or violate the spirit of the American system. They thought of their actions as

Thomas Jefferson did when he made the Louisiana Purchase. The deal violated his strict construction conceptions but it was necessary to guarantee that time's equivalent of "national security."

It should be said further that only rarely was there significant political opposition to or even serious criticism of this unprecedented concentration of executive power. The Supreme Court upset President Truman's use of emergency power to seize the steel plants, and Senator Taft forced him to abandon plans for drafting striking railroad workers. But these were the rare exceptions, and concerned more or less domestic matters. The Congress was an especially weak reed. Willingly acceding to presidential requests for more power, Congress often gave beyond what was asked for. There was almost nothing Congress would not agree to in the name of defense or anti-communism.

There are several reasons for Congress' acquiescence. One was bipartisanship in foreign policy. Although the principle that "politics stops at the water's edge" has a long American tradition, it had applied heretofore to wartime and/or comparable, transient periods of crisis. When, after World War II, Senator Vandenberg brought the Republicans behind the essentials of the Truman Cold War foreign policy, he did so, of course, because he regarded the postwar situation as a critical confrontation with the Soviet Union. It was a natural enough stance for the conservatives of both parties, but the liberals also supported "winning the Cold War" at almost any cost. Even as late as the Democratic resurgence of 1960 the caveat of the Kennedy Administration was not that there was too much executive power, but that it was not being utilized with sufficient vigor. As far as prosecution of the Cold War was concerned, the traditional political processes virtually ceased to function.

All this was quite in harmony with the mood prevailing in the country as a whole. To a considerable extent, to be sure, the unchallenged use of sweeping executive power created the feeling of crisis. Successive administrations followed the advice offered by Senator Vandenberg in 1947: "Scare hell out of the American people." The news media went along, its members frequently considering themselves less reporters of the facts than soldiers of the Cold War. When *The New York Times* withheld news of the impending Bay of Pigs operation out of deference to "national security," it was acting quite in conformity with the journalistic mores of the time.

Thus the executive branch of government—led but by no means always controlled by the president—came to have virtually unlimited power, countered neither by political opposition nor by public criticism, exercising its authority in a milieu which justified its use. Absolute power, Lord Acton said, corrupts absolutely. The nearly absolute power of the executive in the United States over a quarter-century has been no exception. The corruption was not only in the process but also in the policies it produced.

Vietnam provided the comeuppance. The Pentagon Papers spread out for all to see the record of how the vast foreign policy-military establishment acted on fallacy after fallacy as it plunged ahead to the dead-end some of its own leaders privately foresaw—but never publicly protested. First "victory"—never meaningfully defined—was the objective. Then, not being defeated. Then, trying to give the appearance of not being defeated. By the time the Watergate scandals broke upon the country there were increasing doubts as to whether the King actually had any clothes on.

Most observers now agree that the Cold War period resulted in a grave distortion of the American constitutional system. It is an ironic footnote that some of the worst abuses occurred under the Nixon Administration even as it began to move toward détente with the former Cold War enemy. In any case, it seems clear that we will have to put the Cold War psychology behind us once and for all if we are to return to a constitutional system that functions as the framers originally intended.

In this concluding volume of the *Pacem in Terris III* series, the basic questions of constitutional balance of powers, of partisanship in foreign policy, of secrecy, and of the role of the media are explored in the context of contemporary pressures and demands by those directly involved in the process—primarily politicians and journalists.

I

CHECKS AND BALANCES: THE EXECUTIVE VERSUS THE CONGRESS

Certain tensions between the President and Congress in regard to foreign policy are inherent in the American system, if only because, as Governor Tugwell points out in his remarks at the beginning of this chapter, the Constitution is not very explicit about it. The fact is, however, that the formulation and conduct of foreign policy has come to be regarded as an almost exclusively executive function. Theoretically Congress has the ultimate say through its control of the purse strings, and the requirement for Senate approval of treaties and the exclusive power to declare war. But only theoretically.

The illusory character of control through appropriations was demonstrated as far back as Theodore Roosevelt's Administration. When "T.R." decided to make a show of American power by sending the fleet around the world, Congress refused to grant the money for such a voyage. So the President sent the fleet half way around the world, using funds already available to him, and then asked Congress if it wished to leave our navy there. The necessary funds were quickly approved. Control by approval or disapproval of treaties—which were once the main instrumentality of foreign policy—has been obviated by the use of "executive agreements," which serve all the same practical purposes without the formality of the Senate's advice and consent. And the power to declare war lost much of its meaning in an age of "undeclared wars."

Senator Ervin is perhaps best known to Americans as the somewhat avuncular chairman of the Senate Watergate Investigating Committee. He is also recognized in Congress as the leading constitutional expert on the division of powers in the federal government. In his presentation at Pacem in Terris III, *Senator Ervin makes a sweeping assertion that the congressional role in foreign policy should not be merely equal to that of the President but dominant. He argues that under the Constitution Congress was assigned "the primary responsibility for determination of substantive foreign policy," and that the President's role "is primarily representative and instrumental."*

This view constitutes an almost complete departure from what has become the generally accepted norm of relations between Congress and the Executive in regard to foreign policy. Although just how it might be put into practice is unclear, it is indicative of a widespread feeling on Capitol Hill that Congress must somehow reassert its authority. Senator Ervin's answer is to require congressional approval of all executive agreements as a necessary first step.

Advice and/or Consent

Rexford G. Tugwell

The Constitution is somewhat less than clear about responsibility for the shaping and conduct of foreign policy. It says that the President shall make treaties and appoint foreign officers "by and with the advice and consent of the Senate." Washington, the first President, took the word "advice" seriously and thought it meant that he should consult. When an Indian treaty was in question, he went to the Senate chamber and sought the advice he understood he might ask for. He was received coldly. He was told that if he would leave the papers he had brought with him they would be referred to a committee and would be considered in due course.

Washington was furious. He protested that this procedure defeated every purpose he had had in going there; and afterward is reported to have used some of that language he was famous for when enraged.

He never tried to consult again, and none of his successors have risked such a repulse. They have waited until negotiations have been completed and then have made formal submissions. This has not meant that no advice has been given, but at best it has come from a few Senators invited to the White House; and at worst it has been offered in speeches on the Senate floor, taking exception to the result of already-completed negotiations.

This has perhaps preserved the formality of separated powers, but it has ignored the intention that there should be cooperation in the fixing of policies having to do with foreign relations. Presidents, ever since, have got their advice from other sources; and the Senate has more and more been expected to support or reject rather than consult, a tendency certain to result in irritation and critical public comment.

We have seen, in recent years especially, that foreign policies shaped without consultation are likely to lack the support they must have to become effective, and, when they lead to conflicts requiring costly sacrifices, the resulting dissensions can lead to disaster.

The remedy for this situation requires changed attitudes in the executive branch since its initiative may well lead to commitments it would be most embarrassing to repudiate; but it also requires the active realization by Senators that the advice spoken of in the Constitution is something more than formal questionings of department heads by committees and the subsequent issuance of reports.

It may be true, as is often said, that the President has no peers who may share his decisions; but it seems quite clear that, concerning foreign policies, the framers meant to furnish him with some.

Rexford G. Tugwell is a Senior Fellow of the Center for the Study of Democratic Institutions. He served as a member of President Franklin D. Roosevelt's "brains trust," and Governor of Puerto Rico.

Foreign Affairs and Separation of Powers

Sam J. Ervin, Jr.

When the delegates to the Constitutional Convention gathered in Philadelphia in 1787 to draft a Constitution for the new American Republic, an almost universal determination prevailed among these delegates to circumscribe the authority of the Executive with respect to foreign affairs. The virtually limitless power of the English Crown over foreign affairs and its consequences were very much on the minds of these Americans.

To limit executive authority over foreign affairs and other matters delegated to the federal government by the Constitution, the drafters devised and incorporated into the Constitution the principle of separation of powers. Recent developments in the field of foreign affairs notwithstanding, it is as clear as the noonday sun in a cloudless sky that the Constitution divides the national government's powers in the field of foreign affairs between the Congress and the President, granting to neither such exclusive control over foreign affairs that one can be effective without cooperation from the other.

Unfortunately there are those persons, both in government and in academia, who have so little regard for the principle of separation of powers as to embrace the notion that the so-called "realities" of modern international relations require almost exclusive executive control over foreign policy. They contend that arbitrary executive control of America's foreign policy is the price of survival in this uncertain, nuclear age. While I agree that the political, economic and technological changes over the last fifty years necessitate changes in the institutions and processes by which our foreign policy is formulated and implemented, I do not agree that we are required to abandon constitutional principles, especially the principle of separation of powers, which have served us so well throughout our history. Our constitutional form of government was designed not only to make government feasible and practical but also to guard against the historic temptation and irresistible urge of those who govern to gather and use limitless power over the governed.

In general, it is my opinion that the primary responsibility for the determination of substantive foreign policy rests with the Congress, and that the President is under a duty to administer that policy within the framework established by the Congress. According to my reading of the Constitution and constitutional history, the President's role in foreign affairs is primarily representative and instrumental. There is not one syllable in the Constitution and not one word of verified historical evidence to support the view that the President has broad discretion to act without the collaboration and consent of the Congress in foreign affairs.

The document drafted and ratified as our fundamental instrument of government by these freedom-loving Americans demonstrates conclusively, if not always quite exactly, that the Congress was intended to have significant and sometimes singular powers with respect to the foreign affairs of the national government. Article I gives to the Congress the power "to regulate commerce with foreign nations," historically the basis for American foreign policy. It allocates to Congress the power to "provide for the common defense," "to declare war," "to raise and support armies," "to provide and maintain a navy," "to make rules for the government and regulation of the land and naval forces," and other powers directly related to the making of foreign policy and the conduct of foreign affairs.

Furthermore, in granting to Congress "all legislative powers" and the power over appropriations, the Constitution places in the collective hands of Congress such enormous power as to make the effective creation and implementation of American foreign policy absolutely impossible without congressional cooperation or, at least, acquiesence.

By contrast, the enumerated powers of the President with respect to foreign affairs, set forth in Article II, are few and not as comprehensive, at least on their face. According to Article II, the President is "Commander-in-Chief of the Army and Navy of the United States." He is also therein granted the power—with advice and consent of the Senate—to make treaties and to appoint ambassadors, and he is authorized to "receive ambassadors and other public ministers." He has the duty to see that the laws are faithfully executed and commands whatever other powers may result from the vesting of "executive power" in the presidency.

Despite the documented desire of the Founding Fathers to prevent executive autonomy over foreign affairs and the Constitution's generous grants of power to the legislative branch in this field, developments over the past thirty to forty years have caused many students of American constitutional and political history to doubt that Congress can or should significantly participate in the development, establishment and implementation of American foreign policy. Many citizens have come to believe that, quite simply, American foreign relations are within the domain of the President.

While I agree that the Congress has in fact not exercised effectively its considerable powers with respect to foreign affairs, I certainly do not agree with the proposition that executive hegemony over the conduct of America's relations with the rest of the world is either necessary for the effective conduct of foreign affairs or an inevitable result of changing historical circumstances to be accepted despite clear constitutional principles to the contrary. Indeed, I share the strongly-held view of the Founding Fathers that, in the area of foreign affairs more than any other, the principle of the separation of powers as incorporated in the Constitution is essential to the maintenance of our republican form of government. When the legislative branch ceases and desists from responsibly and effectively exercising its constitutional powers with respect to foreign affairs, the Republic will come to an end.

For Congress to reassert its proper role as a full and equal partner in the area of foreign affairs, Congress and the public must come to appreciate what has caused the erosion of legislative effectiveness in this field. Unless we know the nature of the disease, we cannot possibly find the proper cure.

One of the problems which Congress has always confronted in exercising its authority with respect to foreign affairs is the nature of foreign affairs itself and the consequential impact of the Constitution's division of foreign affairs powers. With respect to foreign affairs, the Constitution has divided between the legislative and executive branches what is almost an indivisible process. Congressional power to declare war and the President's power as "Commander-in-Chief," for instance, affect each other so directly that it is impossible for either branch to exercise these powers effectively absent the active cooperation or passive acquiescence of the other. And, without congressional willingness to appropriate funds necessary to implement the nation's established foreign policy—designed with or without congressional consultation—no policy can be made effective. Thus, what the Congress and the President can and cannot constitutionally do in foreign affairs has been an issue since George Washington's presidency, in part because of the practical indivisibility of the national government's power over foreign affairs.

Another problem in asserting congressional prerogatives in this area is the somewhat vague and incomplete constitutional language with respect to the granting and separating of foreign affairs powers. If one adopted a very narrow interpretation of the constitutional language enumerating foreign affairs powers to the Congress and the President, there would be many decision-making processes and functions necessary to the conduct of a nation's foreign policy granted to neither the Congress nor the President. And, while the theory of inherent, sovereign power may well supply a reasonable basis for describing the total scope of the national government's foreign affairs power, such a theory offers no assistance in determining whether these unenumerated, inherent functions and processes belong to the Congress or to the President.

The Constitution vests all "legislative powers" in the Congress and all "executive powers" in the President, but this division is inadequate by itself to determine which of the two branches has exclusive or concurrent authority with respect to a particular foreign affairs function not expressly provided for in the Constitution. Even where the Constitution is explicit in granting one branch a foreign affairs power, confusion and conflict have arisen when the other branch asserts a reasonable claim to a related, unenumerated power. This particular difficulty has been manifested in the use of armed force by the President in circumstances "less than war," while only the Congress has the power to declare a war.

Yet another difficulty in determining the precise lines of authority between the Congress and the President has resulted from congressional delegation of vast authority over foreign affairs to the President during the last several decades. Generally, Congress has not only the right but a constitutional duty to set standards for the exercise of delegated authority and can withdraw such authority at any time. In the area of foreign affairs, however, these delegations of power to the President have usually been made with minimum, if any, standards, and presidential execution of these delegated powers is rarely reviewed. One scholar has written " ... from the beginning, reluctant Congresses have felt compelled to delegate to presidents the largest discretion with minimal guidelines to carry out the most general legislative policy." In my opinion this practice of handing over to the President congressional power over foreign affairs without understandable and effective guidelines and effective congressional oversight has not only clouded the constitutional issue of separation of powers but has seriously undermined congressional capacity to participate effectively in the making of foreign policy.

As a result of these dilemmas in analyzing the words of the Constitution with respect to the foreign affairs powers of the national government, and as a consequence of other, important economic and political developments since the founding of our Republic, the constitutional law of foreign affairs has become more and more confused and the presidency more and more powerful in this field of the law. Despite the uncontested and vast congressional powers relating to foreign affairs, the Senate Foreign Relations Committee concluded in 1967 that, "The concentration in the hands of the President of virtually unlimited authority over matters of war and peace has all but removed the limits to executive power in the most important single area of our national life. Until they are restored the American people will be threatened with tyranny or disaster." (Senate Report No. 797, "National Commitments," Foreign Relations Committee, 90th Congress, First Session)

The present day ascendancy of presidential power over foreign affairs was clearly not intended by the Founding Fathers, has no constitutional basis and threatens greatly the capacity of the national government to formulate and execute a foreign policy which truly represents the best interests of our people. Those wise men who drafted the Constitution clearly intended for the foreign policy of the United States to be determined primarily by Congress—a traditional "legislative" function. Theories devised to justify comprehensive executive authority over foreign affairs understandably do not rely on the words of the Constitution which, in the words of Professor Edward Corwin, do no more than " . . . confer on the President certain powers capable of affecting our foreign relations, and certain other powers of the same general kind on the Senate and still other such powers on Congress. . . ."

We cannot look to the third branch, the Judiciary, for a revitalization of the doctrine of separation of powers in the field of foreign affairs. Since the adoption of our Constitution, the Supreme Court has had very few occasions to interpret and apply the separation of powers doctrine with respect to foreign affairs. The opinion written by Mr. Justice Sutherland in the 1936 case of *United States* vs. *Curtiss-Wright Export Corp.*, 299 U.S. 304—the most celebrated Supreme Court decision in this area—confounds more than clarifies. Justice Sutherland's statement that, "The investment of the federal government with the powers of external sovereignty did not depend upon the affirmative grants of the Constitution," 229 U.S. 304(315), signals great confusion as to understanding the Constitution's division of these foreign affairs powers between the executive and legislative branches. The judicial concept of justiciability and the ultimate political nature of this problem will no doubt continue to preclude the courts from offering effective or definitive answers to the questions which must be met.

The restoration of separation of powers in the area of foreign affairs rests directly on the shoulders of Congress. This great principle of government can be revived only if and when the Congress asserts its rightful authority in formulating, implementing, and reviewing the foreign policy of the United States.

There is reason to believe that the legislative branch is awakening to its constitutional duties and its opportunities in foreign affairs. In recent years, a considerable number of bills have been introduced in the Congress to correct the present imbalance of power between the two branches. While I do not subscribe to each of these legislative proposals, I do sense that their introduction and the broad support they receive means an intensified congressional determination that the legislative branch assume its proper and constitutional role in foreign affairs.

One particular abuse of executive power in the area of foreign affairs with which I have been especially concerned as Chairman of the Senate Subcommittee on Separation of Powers is the use of so-called "executive agreements" to circumvent the treaty-making provisions of the Constitution. Article II, Section 2 of the Constitution states that the President " . . . shall have power, by and with the advice and consent of the Senate, to make treaties, provided two-thirds of the senators present concur." The Senate is thereby given at least a "veto" over commitments made by this country pursuant to a treaty with another country. On the other hand, the Constitution does not expressly grant to the President any power to enter executive agreements.

There is no mention whatever of the term "executive agreement" in the Constitution and there is no accepted definition of what constitutes an "executive agreement." The legal basis for the use of executive agreements is unclear at best, and most frequently has been grounded on the argument of "usage"—a legal justification that is not entirely satisfactory. As I have often noted in various other contexts, murder and rape have been with us since the dawn of human history, but that fact does not make rape legal or murder meritorious. In effect, reliance on "usage" in this instance grounds concepts of constitutionality on acquiescence rather than on the written document, and is, to my mind, wholly unacceptable. It always has been my view that the Constitution means what it says. Moreover, I am not impressed with the recitation of so-called precedents to support *de facto* constitutional amendments. Even 200 years cannot make constitutional what the Constitution declares is unconstitutional.

There has been a considerable, and in my opinion unfortunate, increase in the use of "executive agreements" as an instrument of American foreign policy in the past few decades. As recently as 1930, the United States concluded twenty-five treaties and only nine executive agreements. In 1968, the United States concluded sixteen treaties and 266 executive agreements. By January 1, 1972, the United States had a total of 947 treaties and 4,359 executive agreements. These figures indicate that significant decisions affecting American foreign policy are being made by the executive branch without effective congressional participation in the decision-making process. The executive agreement may be a legitimate method for the President to carry out foreign policy established jointly by the President and the Congress. The extensive use made of this instrument in recent years, however, demonstrates that it is not only being used for administrative convenience but, intended or not, has the effect of circumventing the Congress as an equal partner in making foreign policy.

In an effort to reduce the trend of by-passing the Congress in the making of international agreements and to implement the spirit of Article II, Section 2 of the Constitution, I have introduced legislation which would provide for congressional review of executive agreements. The bill, S.1472, is simple in its terms. It recognizes that the Founding Fathers' concept of shared powers in the area of international agreements has been substantially eroded by the use of so-called executive agreements. In plain language, the measure defines "executive agreements" and requires that the Secretary of State shall transmit each such agreement to both houses of Congress. If, in the opinion of the President, the disclosure of any such agreement would be prejudicial to the security of the United States, the bill provides that it shall be transmitted to the Committee on Foreign Relations of the Senate and the Committee on Foreign Affairs of the House of Representatives under an appropriate injunction of secrecy. Under this injunction of secrecy, only the members of both houses of the Congress shall be permitted to inspect the document.

The bill further provides that each executive agreement transmitted to the Congress shall come into force and be made effective after 60 days—or later if the agreement so provides—unless both houses pass a concurrent resolution expressing disapproval of the executive agreement between the date it is transmitted to the Congress and the end of a 60-day period. In other words, the Congress, in its shared-power role, will have an opportunity to state that it does not approve of an executive agreement during the 60-day period after the agreement is transmitted to the Congress.

It appears to me that the executive branch of the government would welcome a method whereby the Congress would share the responsibility for making international agreements which affect the international image of our nation and its people, the allocation of our tax resources, and, in many instances, impinge upon the possibilities of achieving peace in the world.

What the Congress does in response to excessive executive power over foreign affairs, in the case of executive agreements and with respect to many other matters, will in great measure determine whether the Constitution's intended division of power between the executive and legislative branches in this field will survive. The Constitution has expressly given great authority in the area of foreign affairs to the Congress. There can be little doubt that it gives to Congress the primary responsibility for the determination of substantive foreign policy. It is the very special duty of Congress, mandated by the Constitution's unenumerated and implied congressional powers over foreign affairs, to make certain that our nation's foreign policy is responsive to the wishes of the people. In a democratic society, no policy—especially foreign policy—can long survive without the consent and support of the people.

Thus, Congress possesses not only the constitutional basis for asserting a vigorous role in the development and implementation of American foreign policy, but also carries a sacred constitutional duty to insure that the fundamental notion of separation of powers remains a vital and effective principle in the exercise of the national government's awesome powers in the field of foreign affairs.

Sam J. Ervin, Jr. is a U.S. Senator from North Carolina, Chairman of the Senate Select Subcommittee on Presidential Campaign Activities and the Senate Subcommittee on Separation of Powers.

II

THE PARTISAN ROLE IN
FOREIGN POLICY
– A DISCUSSION

The role of political partisanship in foreign policy, as well as the relationship between the legislative and the executive branches, is here discussed by five of the nation's outstanding political leaders. All of them have been—if they are not still—presidential candidates, and all have had direct concern with foreign policy in the Senate or the Department of State.

The Senators agree that Congress itself has been mainly responsible for the development of top-heavy executive powers, and they are agreed also that it is now time for Congress to redress the balance. Senator Humphrey suggests vastly increased congressional staff aid as a means to that end. Senators McGovern and Muskie call for a reassertion of partisanship—in the highest sense of that term—in foreign policy and cite some hurdles which must be overcome in order to succeed. Senator McCarthy wryly notes that in the 1968 presidential primary campaign his demands for curtailment of presidential power brought the criticism that he favored a "weak presidency." One of the lessons he hopes we have learned from the past few years is that "immoral and dishonest methods used overseas do not stay there" but come home to roost.

Governor Rockefeller, pointing to the relationship between domestic problems and foreign policy, discusses

17

*the kind of understanding and leadership needed to cope
with both. The participants also spoke in response to
remarks circulated in advance by Harry S. Ashmore,
president of the Center for the Study of Democratic
Institutions, who served as chairman of the panel.*

Harry S. Ashmore:

From 1948, when a splinter party led by Henry Wallace unsuccessfully challenged the Cold War postulates of the Truman Doctrine, until 1968, when public reaction against the Vietnam war culminated in President Johnson's decision not to stand for re-election, American foreign policy could be said to enjoy bi-partisan support—or at least to be free of effective partisan attack.

"Our [Cold War] policy was formed without constructive adversary proceedings," writes Chairman J. William Fulbright of the Senate Foreign Relations Committee. In the McCarthy era those within the government who challenged the fundamentals of containment theory and practice were driven from the service or otherwise silenced by charges of pro-communism. In the election campaigns, and in the actions of Congress, the leadership of both parties accepted the dictum that politics stops at the water's edge.

Under the stress of the Vietnam stalemate, this bi-partisan accord has deteriorated. A popular anti-war movement gained significant political strength and demonstrated it in the 1968 elections; in the Senate critics of Administration policy demanded immediate withdrawal of all American troops in Vietnam and re-examination of the policies that led us there; important elements in the mass media have cited a "credibility gap" between government pronouncements on Vietnam and the facts as they were reported from the field; and in the 1972 presidential campaign seven of the eight declared candidates for the Democratic nomination inveighed against the Republican President for his failure to end the fighting in Indochina.

Such divisions on foreign policy continue to be evident within the major parties, reflected in the consternation of the Republican right wing over President Nixon's moves to re-open relations with China and pursue arms limitation agreements with the Soviets, and the in-fighting among Democrats after the collapse of the pro-Vietnam faction led by Lyndon Johnson.

The tension between Congress and the Administration has produced sustained criticism of the concentration of foreign policy formulation and execution in the White House, U.S. aid and development programs, the vast expansion of the armed services with its intimations of a "military-industrial complex," the clandestine activities of the CIA, and the exercise of executive privilege to withhold pertinent information from Congress and the public. This has reached a point where it is now characterized by some leading Senators as a constitutional crisis involving division of powers and responsibility between the executive and legislative branches.

These shifting patterns in reaction to foreign affairs issues may be seen as both the product and the cause of a change in American popular attitudes. The evident pre-eminence of the United States in military and economic capacity at the end of World War II was the dominant factor in the new world order, and a principal source of the ebullient self-confidence with which Americans assumed the burden of world leadership. Now the disillusioning impact of the stalemate in Vietnam is generally acknowledged to have affected citizens of all political persuasions.

The failures in our foreign/military policy have much to do with the marked decline of authority at all levels of government, and to the deterioration of public services. It has been accompanied by, and has contributed to a reshuffling and recasting of the interest groupings that shape electoral politics, although this has not yet been clearly reflected in a national election.

Conservative political leaders have proceeded on the assumption that domestic tensions would diminish with the end of the war, and that the consequences would not go beyond the relatively constrained adjustments in foreign policy manifest in President Nixon's recognition of a new pluralism in the world power balance. The overwhelming defeat of the Democratic candidate in the 1972 presidential contest appeared to sustain that view. While Senator George McGovern hardly could be identified with the radical revisionists, he was one of the consistent senatorial critics who had long seen Vietnam as the essential end product of the Cold War. He attacked not only the American presence in Indochina but the supporting diplomatic and military policies that survive as the basis of the limited redefinition of the national interest embodied in the Nixon Doctrine.

While the McGovern bid failed, it is by no means clear that his defeat indicated rejection of the thesis that the United States has gone wrong in both foreign and domestic affairs because it placed its ultimate, and often its primary reliance on the unilateral exercise of its military power. To successfully carry on this role in a period of massive and rapid change the nation has had to maintain something close to a permanent war footing, a stance that required not only a vast and influential military establishment, but a degree of national unity sufficient to sustain demands for collective and individual sacrifice.

A year into President Nixon's second term there is widespread doubt that this kind of popular support still exists. Indeed, in retrospect there is reason to doubt that majority public opinion ever reflected an attitude more affirmative than passive acquiescence to the virtually unchallenged assertion of the nation's leaders that a world-wide communist monolith constituted a clear and present danger to the national security.

There was no protest so long as the price of guns did not affect the supply of butter, and American troops shed no blood in the course of their foreign duty. A generation that had experienced a shooting war was not moved by the mere inconvenience of those caught up in non-combatant military deployment around the globe, and sharp memories of prewar depression conditioned them to accept the thesis that unprecedented peace-time military spending contributed to the general prosperity. But complacency ended with escalation of the war in Vietnam; the abstractions of the Truman Doctrine were translated into matters of personal concern, and protest mounted in proportion to increases in the draft and the casualty lists.

As the inconclusive fighting dragged on it became increasingly difficult to gloss over the connection between foreign/military policy and the wide variety of domestic dislocations that plagued the nation. That connection, of course, runs both ways, and there can be no doubt that the new formulations of the Nixon Doctrine represent a response to pressures from the home front, as well as recognition of new patterns of power politics emerging overseas.

The Nixon Doctrine's emphasis on the condition that the recipient of American support must "assume the primary responsibility for providing the manpower for its defense" is a case in point. Whether or not they support the manner in which President Nixon has sought disengagement in Vietnam, a heavy majority of Americans is now recorded in the opinion polls as opposing any similar military intervention anywhere in the world. Popular resistance to foreign adventuring shows no signs of being tempered by the wind-down of direct U.S.

intervention in Indochina. It may well be that, whatever his personal disposition may be, adverse public opinion will prevent any future American president from delivering on the pledges embodied in the mutual defense pacts left over from the Cold War.

Domestic discontent could have a similar effect on aspects of foreign policy related to the nuclear deterrent. It is now generally agreed that the prime cause of inflation is the failure of the Johnson and Nixon Administrations to raise taxes to offset increases in defense spending. Although the spiraling cost of living has become an acute political issue, President Nixon continues to support the Pentagon's insistence on still further improvements in the nation's military capacity. Offsetting any savings anticipated from the end of the fighting in Vietnam, or from the arms limitations that may result from the SALT negotiations, the President submitted an actual increase in the defense budget for 1973. With the President's endorsement, the Secretary of Defense notified Congress that he and the Joint Chiefs of Staff would not support accords reached by the President in Moscow unless they were given twenty-five billions to breed a new nuclear arsenal of weapons not covered by the agreement.

The political effect of this is to demand of a restive electorate still more sacrifice on behalf of a military establishment already in disrepute because of dubious command decisions in Vietnam; recurring scandals in military procurement; abuse of security procedures to present an overblown picture of military success and to cover up tragedies like the Mai Lai massacre; wholesale corruption involving military personnel and civilians in the rear areas of Vietnam and the garrison towns of Europe; and the decline of troop morale evidenced by widespread use of drugs and by racial tension.

A President in a stronger position of leadership than that presently enjoyed by Mr. Nixon would have difficulty maintaining the blank-check appropriations for the military that have characterized the Cold War era. Moreover, there is a growing concern among experts in and out of government over the patently inadequate institutional response to rapidly changing and obviously interrelated aspects of foreign and domestic policy. The Pentagon Papers and other documents providing an inside view of the military/diplomatic decision-making process reveal an internal inability to accommodate adverse information or policy dissent, and a growing tendency to block out external criticism and policy intervention by employing classification procedures to obstruct congressional oversight and manipulate public opinion.

The revisionists tend to the view that American foreign policy is shaped in large part by economic interests represented in the misshapen conglomerate called since Eisenhower's day "The Military-Industrial Complex." There can be no doubt that the military suppliers, and their labor unions, use the leverage of their campaign contributions and their capacity to create jobs to exert an often dominant influence in the Congress as well as the executive branch. But there is an abstract force that also keeps many practicing politicians locked to the military/diplomatic status quo. George Kennan has said of the U.S.-Soviet confrontation:

> ... today the military rivalry, in naval power as in nuclear weaponry, is simply riding along on its own momentum, like an object in space. It has no foundation in real interests—no foundation in fact, but in fear, and in an essentially irrational fear at that. It is carried, not by any reason to believe that the other side *would*, but only with the hypnotic fascination with the fact that it *could*. It is simply an institutional force of habit.

Beyond any question of ideology, personality, or partisanship lies the question as to whether this condition is structural. And to those who have been, and may be candidates for President it raises the central issue of whether the formulation and execution of foreign policy should be, and can be immune to the normal working of the democratic process.

We have been caught up in a series of crises that were effectively unanticipated because they fell between governmental stools. Nowhere below the level of the White House does there exist the authority to reach across the bureaucratic channels to pull the policy strands together, and even with the steady expansion of the presidential staff it is hardly possible to make room on the agenda until a crisis is well advanced. The first lesson of the immediate past must be that our decision-making process has become isolated from the public interest as the mass of citizens would define it.

Harry S. Ashmore is President of the Center for the Study of Democratic Institutions.

Hubert H. Humphrey:

The very essence of politics in a democratic society is the honest and forthright discussion of what individuals, groups or parties believe to be the priorities of a country, the allocation of resources, and the formulation of policies and principles of national security. This is what politics ought to be about. For what do we spend our money? What do we consider to be the most important areas of our activity? How do we view national security? Is is to be found only in the military, or are we to view national security as but the cutting edge of a total philosophical and economic commitment?

Senator Ervin has posed the issues very well for us in a remarkable presentation of the constitutional history as it relates to the separation of powers. And let me say very openly at the beginning that separation of powers in government is unique in the American political system. We have to disassociate our thinking from the normal parliamentary structure of government. Separation of powers also requires more than a statement of it; it requires the substance of it. And I shall direct my commentary toward that.

The branches of government are not co-equal simply because one says so. The Congress of the United States is guilty beyond the shadow of a doubt of permitting and indeed acquiescing in and becoming a part of the imbalance of power that now exists between the executive and the legislature. It would be to our own misfortune if we were led to believe that bipartisanship would deny us the right of legitimate debate. Bipartisanship requires ventilation of ideas, hopefully the effective presentation of a point of view. And even bipartisanship requires a continuity on the part of the respective parties or political forces to the commitment that they believe is right. There is nothing wrong in having a minority being able to pursue its course even though it may momentarily have lost out to a majority in the establishment of policy. This is what it's all about in our so-called open society.

Matters of trade policy are bipartisan, and they also ought to be, may I say, a part of legitimate discussion and debate between the executive and the legislative branches. It is so designed in the Constitution. I would hope that we would not feel that the Congress of the United States should have nothing to say except in broad, platitudinous phraseology about trade policy. Surely executive agreements, as discussed this morning by Senator Ervin, require congressional consideration, and treaty-making and national security and defense policies are at the very heart of it. I believe that we had a demonstration very recently here in the Senate of the United States, on the issue of the military procurement bill, of honest differences between the Congress on the one hand and the executive branch on the other. I do not believe that that debate on military procurement injured our security at all. In fact, it possibly enlightened more people about the defense establishment than at any time in recent years. It was necessary to do so.

We've heard a great deal already about why we are in this situation of the increase in executive power. Just let me say that since World War II, indeed starting with World War II, it has been the feeling of the Congress that more and more of the powers must be given to the President. I want to repeat again, it isn't as if the President, whoever he may be, has stolen something. It is that we have given it. I think that has to be made clear to the American people. Whenever we had a tough decision in the Congress over the years, we have generally resolved it by pious pronouncements or some kind of strident rhetoric, and then we've said we'll leave it to the President. We've said, if in your discretion you find it in the national interest to do this or not to do this, Mr. President, you may do it. This is merely a way, I say, of copping out, rather than facing up to the problems.

Now, let me just wind it up here and talk to you about the structure of Congress. The Congress of the United States has made the executive branch of this government powerful by its appropriations and the statutory law that is adopted. The Congress of the United States will provide limousines, bars, and buildings and everything for the executive branch, and prides itself on having lousy food, poor cafeterias, inadequate parking and poor staffing for itself in the name of some kind of prudence or in some kind of economy. We've had a big battle this year on the issue of the budget. We're bound to lose it, at least up to now. Why? Because the executive branch comes in armed literally in military terms with the atomic bomb. We start the fight with firecrackers. We have a handful of people in the two committees of Congress on appropriations to stand up against 1,000 professionals in the Office of Budget and Management. And further, by diffusion of power in the Congress as compared to the one voice of the presidency, we generally lose the battles in public opinion. I have been in both branches of the government. And I know why the executive branch can literally roll the Congress. They come with the experts, the research, the material, the manpower, the advanced planning. They are not after the facts, they're looking ahead; they're ahead of us all the time. We are responding to executive initiatives, and they have a new initiative by the time we're responding to the old one. This is part of the problem. We don't need to have it this way. It isn't as if it is impossible to correct it.

I'm asking the Congress of the United States, if it says it's a co-equal branch and wants to participate in bipartisanship, if it wants to participate in the most sensitive, the most overwhelmingly important area of our entire process of government called national security and foreign policy, to equip itself for the job and quit going around whining and complaining about our inadequacy or being shut out. Let me make one positive, hopefully constructive, suggestion. The executive branch has the National Security Council. There should be an equivalent body in Congress—a joint committee on national security in the House and the Senate of the top leadership, including the elected leadership of the House and the Senate, the top ranking leadership of the prominent committees in the fields of national security, appropriations, foreign affairs, and in the areas of armed services and the Joint Committee on Atomic Energy. There ought to be one place, one board, so to speak, where the executive branch can be cross-examined, where they can't play us off one against another.

I've been in this government for twenty-five years, and I have watched the executive branch come in and give a different song in the Armed Services Committee than they give in the Foreign Relations Committee. I've watched them approach their friends in the House differently than they approach them in the Senate. I think the time is at hand when the executive branch in the area of foreign policy should be cross-examined in one place: one place to state its point of view, one arena in which they can be heard, one forum in which they can be judged. If you want this, you better back us. It is going to cost you some money, but in the long run it will save you some money.

Let me give you an example. We complain about foreign aid. I serve on the Committee on Foreign Relations. We do not monitor foreign aid, we just gripe about it. We do not go into the field to examine what is happening. We just complain about what we read about it in the press. Or if we have to make a trip somewhere and we find somebody goofing off over here or there, or spending money that ought not to be spent, we come back and complain about it. We have no systematic way in the Congress of the United States, week in and week out, month in and month out, to monitor the programs that we authorize and fund. And until we start the monitoring process we're going to be a squeaky wheel, always stuck in the mud but never ever getting any place.

We just passed the War Powers Act, which is a determined effort on the part of the Congress—one of many that have been referred to—to have some sharing of responsibility and also to put on some brakes. First of all, a man who occupies the presidency has almost unlimited power. I don't think the American people have come to realize that it is the most powerful office in the world. The greatest task of that man in that office is to restrain the use of power, not to accumulate more of it. And there are no series of laws or agreements or regulations that are as compelling or as controlling as the character of the occupant. That is the most important thing that we have in American public office.

This Administration has said that it wants to share responsibility with the Congress. It has said that it wants a working partnership. And yet, the War Powers Act, which is the product of several years of intensive work on the part of the Congress itself, is today under the shadow of a veto. I submit that if the President of the United

States really believes what he says, if he really believes that there ought to be active and meaningful participation by the Congress in the basic foreign policy decisions, he will not veto this bill. What we're talking about is the question of war or peace, because presidential power has permitted and indeed has authorized and initiated what we call presidential wars. If we're going to put the brakes on, and if we're going to share in the responsibility, then there has to be a willingness on the part of the executive to take a new look, to venture into possible new areas of understanding between Congress and the presidency. I hope that the President will not veto this major effort on the part of the Congress of the United States to bring Congress into the sharing of the responsibility on the questions of peace and war. If the President does veto it, then it is but another sign that there are those who never seem to forget and never seem to learn.

Hubert H. Humphrey is a U.S. Senator from Minnesota and former Vice-President of the United States.

George McGovern:

Senator Ervin told us one of his famous preacher stories, but he didn't tell my favorite Ervin preacher story. This is the one of the aging minister who is attempting to explain the development of the human race to a class of young people. He went through the creation of Adam and Eve and said from this union came Cain and Abel and so on through the development of humankind. A hand went up in the rear of the room and a young man said, "Reverend, where did Cain and Abel get their wives?" There was kind of an embarrassed pause, and then the old minister said, "Young man, it's questions like that that are hurtin' religion." This is that kind of age of doubt and questioning. It's also, I think, an age of paradox. Perhaps nothing is more paradoxical than Senator Jackson earnestly quoting a Soviet communist as the chief witness for his legislative initiative. There is a legitimate relationship between the subject of Soviet-American détente and the question of human liberty. But the relationship that exists between détente and our continuing support for dictators in Southeast Asia is a relationship that escapes me entirely. While I'm very much concerned about the subject of human liberty in the Soviet Union, I think all of us would approach that task with less anxiety if it were not for the tragic fact that we go there with so much blood on our own hands from this long and tragic involvement in Southeast Asia.

The premise that politics stops at the water's edge, which is a premise we're challenging here, is one that I think both violates our democratic form of government and also violates the most enduring traditions of this country. It is really a false and dangerous doctrine. Partisanship usually conjures up in our minds the image of a person who is willing to put narrow personal or party advantage ahead of the national interest. But I use the term here today not to characterize the phrase in that manner but to describe deep-seated and honest differences of opinion that need to be fully aired on important public questions, and especially on those all important areas of war and peace. Some of the finest moments in the history of American foreign policy have been marked by sharp partisan debate in that sense of the word. The debates that took place between the Whigs and the Democrats over the Mexican War in the late 1840s is a case in point. The debates around the turn of the century over whether or not we should take over the colonies of Spain was perhaps a high point in foreign policy discussion. And in our own day the mounting congressional and public criticism of U.S. involvement in Indochina, more than anything else, has forced a change in both the previous Administration and in this Administration in our policy in that part of the world.

The uncomfortable fact is that for most of the last quarter of a century the fear of communist power abroad and the invoking of a bipartisan response here at home has had the effect of stifling necessary public debate. As Senator Humphrey has said so well, the Congress must bear a major part of the responsibility for acquiescing in that effort to stifle public discussion of important foreign policy questions. In the bipartisan search for national security Congress not only yielded vital constitutional powers to the executive branch, but it permitted foreign policy managers to engage in secretive and inhumane and illegal activities abroad. And I believe that the "dirty tricks" of Watergate that we are now reading about actually had their seedbed in twenty-five years of conditioning to the view that anything goes as long as you put a national security label on it and aim at your enemies, either at home or abroad. True partisanship, let me emphasize, does not mean party allegiance; rather it connotes the willingness to dissent from public policy either behind or beyond the water's edge.

In the War Powers Act, Congress has approved a first step towards reasserting its war power. We might debate the wisdom of the form that step took, but at least it was some manifestation that Congress is reaching out to reassert its powers in the area of war and peace. It is also some indication that members of Congress are more willing to subject themselves to criticism in speaking out on foreign policy questions. As one of those critics who, over the years, has been censured for challenging our posture abroad, I reject here the notion that citizens must rally behind misguided policy in the name of national security. If patriotism under dictatorial rule means a kind of blind loyalty to the ruler, patriotism in a democracy includes the obligation on the part of members of Congress and members of the public at large to speak out against those courses of action that one believes does not serve the national interest. This is the higher patriotism, and we can offer no less.

George McGovern is a U.S. Senator from South Dakota.

Nelson Rockefeller:

This panel discussion here and the forthrightness and the frankness of the expression are perfect illustrations of why I am sure that I share with you a tremendous sense of confidence and optimism about the future of this great land of free men. Let me now briefly make an analysis of the subject as I see it before us. The inherent tension between Congress and the executive branch of government has been argued since the Constitutional Convention in 1787. It is a debate which has become particularly acute at times of strong executive action, which is necessarily focused on specific issues. At present some of these issues are in the area of foreign policy, centered upon the president's power to conduct war and include executive agreements in lieu of treaties. Without detracting from the importance of this debate, we must recognize that the very specificity of the issues tends to obscure the breadth and the significance of the problem really confronting us. That problem is America's inability to define its national interests in terms acceptable to the nation's and commensurate with its international interests.

Our current difficulty in defining America's national interests cannot be explained by any simple consideration of the different vantage points of the executive and the legislative branches. Nor can it be resolved by legislation, which can only cope with the manifestations of the problem. Rather it is imperative that we address the real causes of our malaise—the basis of our inability to identify the components of national interest—by broadening our perspective and coming to terms with two essential problems which challenge us. First, the impact of the nature of changes which face us, both domestically and internationally; and second, the interrelation between our domestic situation and the concept of foreign policy. Unless the current debate is viewed in this broader context, the nation is in danger of resolving issues through cosmetics rather than real solutions. We are all aware of the impact of change in our daily lives. But our perceptions of the forces and the implications of change are indistinct. Nonetheless, we're beginning to assess the nature of the changes that have taken place and are taking place and to judge their effect not only upon our own lives as individuals but upon our institutions and upon our political structures. Let me list some of these.

The most profound shifts have been taking place. First, it is becoming increasingly less possible to isolate domestic problems from foreign affairs. As examples, consider the energy crisis, national security, the balance of payments problem, interest rates, food shortages and spiraling prices. Second, the United States has undergone a change in its world position. Although America's decline in strength has been in relative terms, the ramifications of this shift have been both external and internal in their repercussions. Third, the nature of our problems has become complicated by the emergence and impact of the problems of race, drugs, environment, abortion and welfare. They impinge upon the nation's psyche, and they are, therefore, inherently more explosive than those that faced us in the Thirties. Fourth, technology has brought about instant communication. We're able to witness the immediate result of our policies, of our successes and failures.

Today we must be concerned with the effect of these changes on our political process. Cultural issues have brought about the rise of a new clientele, a clientele that must be absorbed within the existing framework of parties. This process of absorption is straining our political processes, as any witness to the effort to rebuild the structure of our political parties can testify. In addition, many of these value-oriented issues have penetrated the political process by fostering a system of conflicting demands. For example, the public demands a solution to race problems, but resists necessary legislation. Equally the public wants clean environment, but cheap fuel and more cars. The inability to solve these problems has created frustration on both the part of the government and the public, with the politician caught in the middle.

The increasingly blurred line between foreign and domestic policy, coupled with the emergence of new cultural patterns and the relative decline of American power has further contributed to the unwinding of our political processes and the destruction of the cohesion of our society. It is no longer assumed that American action by definition is right. But there is increasingly widespread confusion about what America's moral role really is. This confusion, of course, has led to the questioning of the basis of foreign policy, such as has taken place here at *Pacem in Terris III*. What is its purpose? To preserve American security, to stabilize the international system, or to influence the domestic policies of other nations? While either end may be legitimate, one cannot pursue both successfully at the same time. Thus, in international affairs the same pattern of conflicting demands is emerging. For example, the U.S. is being asked to avoid commitments, but to remain a world leader; and to allocate more resources for internal problems and at the same time maintain a high level of defense. It is questionable that any government could do both.

Technology itself has interjected a new element into our political system. We are all aware that the rise of the televised political activists and demonstrators, the pictures of wartime horrors, have had an immeasurable effect upon all of us. What are the implications for the political process? The visibility of highly dramatic events has increased the vulnerability of politicians and the political system to immediate pressures. In addition, it has tended to define issues in both simplistic and personalistic terms.

While there have been positive results from living room history and Sunday morning quarterbacking, there are negative aspects of this technological change. To remove the shock absorbers built into the political system has created a dangerous government vulnerability in time of crisis. It could encourage an atmosphere in which to avoid confrontation, since the stakes are so high, the leader may avoid taking effective action.

The failure of understanding the causes and anticipating the implications of changes has led, at worst, to a questioning of the validity of the whole system as well as the integrity of American values. At best, this failure has contributed to a loss of cohesion which in the long run could undermine the stable environment necessary to rational decision-making. The loss of cohesion which now threatens us should be our primary concern. Without the creation of a new conceptual framework in which our goals can be defined, we shall not be able to solve our domestic problems. Equally the loss of cohesion and the implied loss of direction will impose an intolerable strain on the international system, since our perception of ourselves, our self-image, not only generates our own behavior but largely determines the conduct of both our allies and our adversaries.

American leaders and public can and must devote themselves to building a new consensus. This can be accomplished, first, by achieving an understanding of the rapid changes that are taking place in the world and concentrating upon the development of policies and concepts which can deal with them; second, by demonstrating the flexibility and ability of our political parties to absorb new directions and to exert discipline upon their members; third, by conducting debate on major issues in an open and responsible manner both within parties and between the parties; and, fourth, by focusing on issues rather than on individuals. The tendency to perceive errors in judgment as the designs of evil men is not only fruitless but debilitating.

Now that we have realized that we cannot solve all the world's problems, we are in danger of convincing ourselves that we cannot solve any of them. This attitude can be more destructive than our over-confidence of the Sixties. But I am confident that it is possible to gain the necessary understanding and perspective of events and, with public participation, to develop a consensus on what needs to be done to reflect our best interests at home and abroad.

Nelson Rockefeller is former Governor of New York and former Assistant Secretary of State.

Edmund S. Muskie:

I was unable to resist thinking, as I listened to Hubert Humphrey, how different things would be now had they turned out differently in 1968. In any event, no one can do a better job of criticizing the Congress than those of us who are members of it. And that's healthy, I suggest. As I contemplate the public attitudes to those of us in political life, I'm reminded of an observation made recently by someone who said that if Patrick Henry thought that taxation without representation was bad, he ought to see what it is like with representation. It is quite clear that no serious challenge to the proposition that foreign policy would benefit from vigorous partisan debate would be raised on this panel. I'm not going to belabor the point, although, unavoidably, I must touch on it. But I'd like to put a slightly different perspective on the problems to which we should address ourselves in this connection.

It is clear that perhaps the pre-eminent problem that America faces today is the erosion of public confidence in our political institutions and in our political leaders. I'm reminded of a story of a gentleman who was mountain-climbing and fell off the edge of a cliff. As he fell, thrashing about, through some miracle he grasped the branch of a tree growing out from a cliff. He hung there, got his breath and then began to shout for help. And at that moment a loud, deep, quiet voice from on high was heard: "My son, let go of the branch." There was no response, and again the deep, quiet voice spoke out: "My son, have confidence in me, let go of the branch." At this point the man looked up and said, "Is anyone else up there?" The erosion of public confidence reaches the highest of places. And the question comes to us, how shall we approach the task of restoring it? Do we restore it by revitalizing our concept of the father figure in the White House? Will he heal our divisions and solve our problems by wisdom of his own making? Or shall we heal them by making this process open to those whose lives are involved in public policy decisions? I think this is the best argument of all for an abandonment of the notion that we do not debate foreign policy.

We are hopefully moving into a more diverse world, certainly a more fragmented world as one looks about, notwithstanding the dominance of two superpowers. And isn't it interesting that the emergence of two superpowers has in a sense given the small nations of the earth more power to influence the course of events, to hamstring the great nations, to tie their hands and to decide for themselves what they shall do about their own parochial local or regional affairs? Now how do we deal with the complexities of problems such as this? The remarks made here by my distinguished colleagues on this panel have been excellent expositions of important points in connection with this debate. The point I want to emphasize and which they made is that America cannot afford to speak, at home or abroad, with just one voice, with respect to the affairs of mankind.

The reason for this difference that we've become accustomed to in dealing with domestic and foreign policy problems, this double standard was reflected in something that Justice Sutherland said in his *obiter dicta* in the 1936 Curtiss-Wright case. He referred to "the plenary and exclusive power of the President as the sole organ of the federal government in the field of international relations . . . " That concept, that America must speak with one voice if it is to be heard and respected, may have had some relevance, may have been a sensible one. During the period of the late Thirties and World War II, a united America was clearly an important condition to the effort to win in the struggle over Nazism. In times of evident danger we do naturally rally about the President as Commander-in-Chief. But I submit, along with my colleagues, that that natural tendency has been carried to the point in the last twenty-five years where it has undermined our real national interests. And it has undermined them because it has discouraged and inhibited dissent on important matters.

We face the task of redefining America's relationships to the rest of the world, of redefining our ambitions for our country and ourselves, and of redefining the uses to which our purposes, our resources and our leadership will be put. What we submit to you here is that that redefinition cannot be accomplished by suppressing criticism of existing policy or its implementation. It cannot be achieved by denying the people and their representatives the information on which official judgments are based. And it can best be reached by a dialogue between those who govern and those who challenge, with the public as the audience and the judge.

The need for such an exchange, I submit, is increased by our present political circumstances. Right now the President's moral authority is badly undermined by the campaign scandals of last year, by the abusive invocation of the national security mystique to sanction common crimes, by the deception and secrecy by which our military strength was committed to and used in Indochina. He is in no position to lead us alone to a new consensus on foreign policy. Thanks to the success of some of his policies—and we must look at the other side of the coin—we may now have the luxury of an interlude from ultimatums, an intermission in the play of tension, when we can take the time to examine our old commitments, outline our new interests, and try to determine a steady course for our policies. I know no way other than through partisan debate to challenge old assumptions, to question current tactics, and to define alternative futures. The goal of such a debate should be agreement that dissolves party lines, but the open discussion is as important as the results it produces.

Internal dialogue within the Administration, joined only by a few respected leaders of the congressional opposition, simply is not good enough. It will not satisfy our need for a foreign policy all Americans can comprehend and at most can support. The obsessive secrecy about our actions abroad, the tendency to say one thing in public and to do something else on the sly has already drained the reservoir of public trust in foreign policy leadership. To restore that trust, an open, thorough and necessarily partisan examination of our behavior and our strength is essential. Thirty years ago Walter Lippmann wrote, "Upon the effects of our foreign policy are staked the lives, the fortunes and the honor of the people, and a free people cannot be asked to fight and bleed, to work and sweat for ends which they do not hold to be so compelling that they are self-evident."

The ends of our present foreign policy are only dimly perceived. To make them compelling again, to unite Americans around a new commitment to international responsibility, we must make foreign policy a topic of public concern, not just secluded in expert consultations. Our public structure is the best instrument we have to foster public debate. We should use it for that purpose, as we have before, to involve the people in the decisions which will shape our future.

Edmund S. Muskie is a U.S. Senator from Maine.

Eugene J. McCarthy:

I would like to add to what Senator Muskie has said and note that I, too, have some reflections on how things might have been different today if they had been different in 1968. In some ways, the point of this conference is more or less where I came in in 1968. In the campaign of that year, the public emphasis was on the war and what we ought to do about it. But we also talked about the power of the presidency and tried to draw attention to that issue and to the over-personalization of the office, and to the danger of abuse, if not actual abuse, of the office as a consequence.

I was rather severely criticized. One of the men who defected from my campaign (with a press conference—and that is a real defection) said that my concept of the presidency would result in a weak presidency. Perhaps. He has just finished a book entitled *The Imperial Presidency*, in which he suggests that the power of the presidency has been overly concentrated.

Our concern here, however, is principally about the process by which foreign policy is determined. I would note at the opening of this discussion that insofar as our involvement in Vietnam is concerned, change in process would not have had much significance. The Congress was quite ready to support that war as it gradually developed. As a test, we—that is, the Congress, or more particularly the Senate—did have two votes on the Tonkin Gulf resolution, one in 1967 when it was proposed that the resolution be brought up for re-examination and discussion. There were only five votes in favor of this action. Then in 1970, when the same resolution was brought up for repeal, the President having said he did not need the resolution, there were only five votes in favor of maintaining the resolution. The process was the same in 1967 as it was in 1970. Neither vote had any significant bearing on how the war was prosecuted.

As I see it, the issue which Senator Ervin brought before us here is not really one of the separation of powers or of the balance of powers, but rather a question of how power and responsibility are to be shared in the government. I am quite convinced that if the men who drafted the Constitution had anticipated a time when foreign policy would be as important as it is today, and a time when we would have a military establishment of the magnitude of the one which we now have, they would have outlined somewhat different procedures for dealing with military and foreign policy. The Constitution was drafted almost as an anti-foreign policy document, and we have lived with those limitations.

I did not realize how much things had changed until, in the last year of my service in the Senate, I received a call from the Spanish Ambassador who said that he would like to come up and talk to me. When he arrived, he said, "I want to talk to you about the Treaty of Utrecht." I said, "Oh, talk about the Treaty of Utrecht? I have not talked about that for a long time. It involved Napoleon?" "No," he said, "It was signed in 1713 at the end of the War of the Spanish Succession. That was the year in which the British got Gibraltar, 250 years ago, and we would like to talk about revising the Treaty." He was most serious. His attitude showed how people thought about treaties in the eighteenth century, the century of the Constitution. A treaty was a commitment which was expected to last. After my opening uncertainty, I recovered a little and said, "But that treaty also raises some questions about succession to the Spanish throne. It would, I believe, cause some trouble for Franco and interfere with his plans." "No," he replied, "the provision about succession was only a codicil." Even in those days, they made exceptions in codicils.

We have come through a century-and-a-half, roughly, dealing and acting under an instrument which was not intended to provide procedures for conducting foreign and military policies such as we now conduct or have been conducting. One can blame presidents for usurping power, or blame Congress—or the Senate, in particular—for giving it away. I think there is fault on both counts, but uncertainty of procedure made its contribution to the confusion. Certainly in the period since the end of World War II, the Senate, which has principal congressional responsibility under the Constitution for participating in the making of foreign policy, did give away power—in large measure, by agreeing to comprehensive treaties—NATO, for example, which, although comprehensive, had some limits, and beyond that, SEATO and other commitments in which there were practically no limitations of time, or geography, or even ideology.

To the credit of President Eisenhower, he never did much that John Foster Dulles recommended, but he did allow the Secretary to go about the world signing us up in almost any place he could find people who would sign and making legal and moral commitments for us. Then Dulles went away but the commitments were left. And Democrats have been trying to honor them ever since. I suppose that John Foster Dulles is the first Secretary of State in our history who had more power after his death than he had while alive and more power in the administrations of the opposite party than he ever had in his own party.

When treaties were not adequate, the Congress passed resolutions just to fill in the gaps, in effect saying,

"Is there anything else you would like, Mr. President? There is a little area here that has not been covered, and we thought you would like to pick up whatever loose power or responsibility is lying around." In most cases, the presidents were willing.

There are two other procedural, historical points bearing on this problem which I think are important. These relate to ideas which are in some cases responsible for the Congress' giving up power and in some cases responsible for its not exercising power when it had it. These two ideas have been, I believe, very mischievous. One is the idea that politics stops at the water's edge—we have all heard that—and morality also. And it is suggested that it also stops at the entrance to the Pentagon and at the gateway to the CIA; that there should be no criticism, or division, that a foreign policy be uncritically supported. This proposition may be all right under some conditions, but the Constitution did not anticipate uncritical acceptance of foreign policy. Special protection against arbitrary foreign policy was built into it.

It was anticipated that the Congress in dealing with domestic problems might be somewhat irresponsible. Presidential veto of congressional action in the domestic field was provided. The Founding Fathers provided that the President could veto the acts of Congress, in effect saying that it would take two-thirds of the Congress to do something that the President did not want done at home. The same Founding Fathers turned things around in the field of foreign policy by providing that treaties, the principal means of determining foreign policy, had to be ratified by two-thirds of the Senate, in each case providing a veto by one branch of the government over the actions of another branch. When it is said that we should have a bipartisan foreign policy, it must mean only that we ought to have a foreign policy which is supported practically unanimously, or at least by two-thirds of the Congress and of the people. This is certainly the way in which President Truman worked out NATO, and the adoption of the United Nations Charter. The support was bipartisan, but that was not the issue. It was that these programs had what was almost unanimous support of the country, not a compromised support. To assert that politics or partisanship should stop at the point of military and foreign policy is to set up conditions for irresponsible foreign policy and conditions which tend to make it almost impossible to stop or challenge such policy once it has been initiated.

The second mischievous idea is a modification of the first. It is that even though partisanship may creep into foreign policy, there should be no criticism from members of the party in power. The slogan then becomes, not my country right or wrong, but my party right or wrong, and even my President, right or wrong.

I have expressed concern in recent years over the way in which Presidents use pronouns. President Johnson used to refer to "my cabinet," "my helicopters," etc. President Nixon is more inclined to use the plural "we" without explanation as to whether it is the papal "we" or the royal "we" or some other that he has not told us about. Occasionally a President refers to himself in the third person.

This is a period of challenge and of re-examination for our country. There are, I believe, three counts on which this re-examination is necessary. The first is military. We have learned the limitations of our military power, a good thing to know. Second, we have learned the limitations of our economic power, also a good thing to know. And third, we have also learned the limitations of our moral power and moral strength, which we have over-estimated to some extent. The most telling comment on this point was one I heard just before the last election when a young man said to me, "President Nixon will be re-elected" (he disappeared, or seemed to, after saying this to me) "because the country will not vote against its own guilt." He may have been right. In any case, that is the best explanation of the election results that I have heard.

In a way, we have had our guilt come back to us and we have had to recognize it. Other nations have done the same. I recall an Englishman talking about the abuse of colonials in England and saying, "We have simply brought our cruelty home." And the French at the time of the Algerian War facing up to their cruelty and saying, in effect, "We will not let that cruelty be brought home or continued in the colony." Our problem and our condition have been made clearer by the defenses made by some of the persons involved in the last campaign. It is evident that immoral and dishonest methods used overseas do not stay there. They come back. It is clear that things cannot be done in the national interest in one place without being used with the same justification in other places. Methods which we accepted as usable against other people have been used against our own.

We have come a long way from George Washington to Richard Nixon, from John Adams to Spiro Agnew, from John Jay to John Mitchell. I hesitate to continue the list. We have come this way in part because we have neglected procedures and processes. The Constitution gives only a few lines to purposes but page after page to processes, to ways and means by which this Republic was to operate.

After nearly 200 years, it is time for us again to give thought not just to the substance of government and of national policies, but also to procedures. It may well be that the historic role of the Nixon Administration has been to reveal to us rather clearly the potential dangers in our government and the possibilities of abuse and of exploitation, to remind us of the warning of men like George Clinton of New York who in 1788-89 warned us that the potential of the Constitution might be such that "If given time, a President, if he wills, can destroy the Republic."

We have not reached that point, but we have seen the dangers. We must turn to the task of caring for the Republic with the spirit expressed by John Adams when he wrote that there was present among the people of the American colonies what he called the spirit of "public happiness" which he defined as a willingness to take public responsibility and civic responsibility. He said that the spirit was so strong that the Revolution was won before it was fought. I believe that that spirit is still within us, but it must be stirred and released.

Eugene J. McCarthy is a former U.S. Senator from Minnesota.

Humphrey:

A point has been made by Senator McCarthy about the Constitution. I would like to point out that what the Constitution says is important, but what it doesn't say is also important, maybe more important than what it says. For example, you can read the Constitution from the Preamble to the last Amendment and there's not one thing in it that is designed to protect the government from the people. But there are many features in it—details, sections and subsections—designed to protect the people from the abusive power of government. It's very important that we remember that. I mention that because now we have been trying to cloak government with a kind of sanctimonious paneling or covering that is supposed to place it beyond the protest or dissent or criticism of people. At least, if criticism comes, it is oftentimes—not generally but oftentimes—looked upon as being abusive or without proper understanding. One thing that we hear much in the executive branch—and it is characteristic of every administration—is that they have the information. They say, if you only know what we know, you would see it our way. I have been on both sides, and I want to tell you that the only difference is that they hire more people on the other side to know what we ought to know.

Going back to what I said earlier, I believe in a strong presidency. I think it would be a terrible mistake for this country not to have what we call a strong presidency. I believe in leadership, and there is a great deal of difference between leadership and dictation. Leadership is persuasion. Leadership is leading; it is not demanding, it is not commanding. A strong presidency becomes an abusive executive office or a corrupted one when its weight is excessive in relationship to other branches of the government. The important thing is balance. We talk about the co-equal branches of government. They are theoretically co-equal, but not practically. It isn't only that Presidents have taken powers; by precedent and tradition they have now accumulated great powers. They had to take those powers from the powers that were delegated to or authorized to the Congress of the United States. And the reason they were taken is because the Congress didn't use them.

Politics is another word for power, and when somebody doesn't use that which belongs to him or to an institution, then it gravitates to someone else. Power is not floating in thin air; it is always being used. In our system, we have tried to use checks and balances, stress and counterstress, as they do in engineering, in order to balance off any possibility of the abuse of power. An effective input on the part of the Congress in foreign policy, which includes debate and dissent and argument, and all that goes with it, cannot be accomplished just by one hundred men in the Senate, and 435 in the House, against two million or more public servants in the executive branch. Congress does not have an information retrieval system and other minimal tools. This same Congress will appropriate hundreds of millions to the Defense Department to update its computer systems for weaponry, for information, for research, or whatever.

Your Congress doesn't have 150 people working on appropriations. We handle an $86 billion authorization for defense with a handful of people. And only recently one of the prominent members of the Senate told me that the whole process for a while was stymied because one of our most important people died.

This is part of the problem, and one of the reasons for it is that in the main the public looks upon Congress as sort of an odd institution. If you want to razz somebody, you razz the Congress. If a Congressman travels, it is a junket. If the Secretary of State goes, it is a vital mission. When Congressmen travel it is very difficult to take staff so that you can do a good job. But I traveled as Vice-President with staff running out of my ears. The Vice-President has some responsibility but no authority whatsoever, but because he travels as a representative of the executive branch he has staff.

We are cowards in the Congress. We will not do for ourselves what we need to do. It's much easier for me to complain about the President than it is to right our own house. For example, the committee structure itself does not lend itself to the twentieth century, and surely not to the twenty-first. Let me give you an illustration. Where would you go to discuss trade policy in the Congress? The executive branch has a separate institution to discuss trade. Peter Flannagan is at the head, and now there are special representatives. It is all tied together. They come in with one purpose and one program. Where do you go in Congress? Well, the House Ways and Means, Senate Finance, the Committees on Commerce. The Committee on Foreign Relations in the Senate doesn't even have a subcommittee on international trade. And yet possibly the most important area of discussion and cooperation and confrontation in the foreseeable future is in the economic sphere in international relations. I don't say that one committee is any better than any other. The point is that we're improperly and poorly structured.

We do not provide ourselves with facilities, including the space in which to live. Come up and see the Senate and House offices. And then go and see what the same Congress does for the executive branch, appropriating money for one building after another. I know this is the nuts and bolts, the nitty-gritty of it. It isn't philosophical. But I've had enough of philosophy. I know what the philosophy is because I've read it all. And I've had a bellyful of it. The fact of the matter is, we are not equipped. We fight the battle against the President on impoundment and we don't even have lawyers for the Congress of the United States. We ought to have a General Counsel. We can't depend on the Department of Justice. We ought to have our own General Counsel. I'm simply saying if you talk about separate divisions of government and checks and balances, what happens is that we give them the checks and they get the balance.

McGovern:

I was very impressed that every speaker here made some reference, not only to the procedures and the processes that we follow in foreign policy formation, but also to the importance of the character of the occupant of the White House and the men and women who make policy in our government. The truth is that the Constitution, even if it were followed line by line, was not designed for men, for government officials, who don't understand the spirit of it. There's no way that you can possibly devise a Constitution to ensure that this country is not going to stumble into wars or deliberately commit itself to conflicts that are a violation of our principles. The Congress is given the power over the purse, but if we surrender that power or if we are determined to use it for goals and priorities that don't serve the national interest, there's no way that can be changed by the Constitution. We need to understand that if we're going to find our way once again, if we're going to recover the public confidence that Senator Muskie referred to, there has to be some union of enduring moral principles with the political procedures in the foreign policy determination of this country.

Muskie:

Perhaps the most significant "amendment" to the Constitution was never submitted to the Congress or to the people. That is the development of television, which has given the President almost exclusive opportunity to speak to the country in matters of foreign and domestic policy. Until we can deal with that problem effectively, the structural changes we make in the Congress or the new relationships we are able to devise between the President and the Congress are not going to work. There is simply no effective way for those who challenge the President's policy to do so with as great visibility or with as loud a voice as he does, with unlimited access to that great medium of television. We have to address ourselves to that problem.

III

THE FOREIGN POLICY ESTABLISHMENT AND THE MEDIA

Foreign policy has traditionally been a more or less elitist concern in the United States. In the period since World War II, our foreign—and military—policies have been managed by a remarkably small group of functionaries with quite similar backgrounds and much the same outlook on America's role in world affairs. Whether in or out of office, they comprised a somewhat exclusive foreign policy club, cutting across and ignoring party lines.

In the period before World War II, when foreign policy was not a major American concern, many American diplomats felt they were regarded by their compatriots as second-class citizens. The traditional American attitude toward all diplomats was long one of suspicion and sometimes disdain. American preoccupation with the Cold War changed all that. Suspicion was focused only on those suspected of being "soft on communism." There were not many such, and few of those survived the McCarthy period. Those in charge of and working in the vast and powerful agencies concerned with prosecuting the Cold War—the men Richard Barnet has called the "crisis managers"—were surrounded by an aura of prestige and high patriotism. A part of this was due to the fact that these men and the activities in which they were involved were "news." There developed an interesting and paradoxical relationship between them and the Washington correspondents who covered them— cooperative and adversarial at the same time. If those concerned with high policy were necessary to the journalists, the journalists were necessary to the policy-makers—both to influence public opinion and for bureau-cratic in-fighting.

These two themes—the foreign policy establishment and the relations of government officials with the news media—are discussed in this section by two experts with eminent qualifications in both areas.

The men who conduct the U.S. foreign policy are discussed by John Kenneth Galbraith, Harvard professor, former U.S. Ambassador to India, author, economist, political philosopher and social critic extraordinary. One of the few "card-carrying liberal" leaders who never accepted the Cold War imperatives, Mr. Galbraith managed to be part of the "foreign policy establish-ment"—at least in the Kennedy years—and a critic of it at the same time. Controversial, as always, here he advances the thesis that the kind of foreign policy pursued is responsible for the kind of men who conduct it. And, paraphrasing the Duke of Wellington, he says the men required by the foreign policy we have had "may not frighten the enemy but, by God, they should frighten us."

The relationship between government and media and its importance in foreign policy is taken up by James C. Thomson, Jr., who, before he became Curator of the Nieman Fellowships for Journalism at Harvard, as an official of the State Department, faced the press on frequent occasions. Here he draws on his own experiences to describe "the courtship" between the press and government officials, which he says is "at best a long-term affair, sometimes a one-night stand but very seldom matrimony." The existence of a free press, Mr. Thomson says, is an obstacle to effective functioning of the executive branch of government, but, he adds, so are Congress and free elections. The press has by no means always done its job adequately, Mr. Thomson feels, but generally speaking he gives it a better rating than the government. If there is conflict between the two, it only shows both are "alive and kicking and, as a result, so is the nation."

Of Men and Foreign Policy

John Kenneth Galbraith

The professional discussion of foreign policy is unique among the great social disciplines in that good tailoring combined with a certain assurance of manner is extensively a substitute for thought. For this reason, even on an occasion that so unites erudition with solemnity as this, one can, with a sense of novelty, still make a commonplace point. It is this: While, as commonly imagined, men do have a certain influence on the foreign policy—on those dealings in and with other countries that affect national and general well-being—policy has an even more profound effect in selecting the people who guide it. This circumstance, I shall argue, does much to specify the kind of policy that we can pursue. There are policies which require a class of talent which we cannot wisely risk or afford. These are matters which even a brief glance at recent history affirms.

The years of World War II and those immediately following were a remarkably compassionate and creative time in the history of American foreign policy. The Charter of the United Nations, the Bretton Woods agreements, UNRRA, the creation of the specialized agencies, and the Marshall Plan all affirm the point. The circumstances of war and reconstruction and the interest in peace, however fugitive, that always follow the experience of war, required a strongly cooperative relationship with other countries, including the Soviet Union.

This policy, in turn, attracted the talents and energy of a remarkable group of men and women—George C. Marshall, the earlier and better Dean G. Acheson, Herbert H. Lehman, W. Averell Harriman, Paul Hoffman, Eleanor Roosevelt, Adlai Stevenson, many others. Nearly all owed their eminence not alone to their perception of the issues but also to their influence with the Congress and the public at large. The policy of the time was accessible to the Congress and the public. Both had to be persuaded. Hard-nosed diplomatic, military and espionage talent was not especially useful for this work. It was, we may also recall, a golden age in American influence and esteem.

In the second Truman Administration, the policy changed. The change was partly in response to the deep mistrust that American conservatives—businessmen and their legal, military and diplomatic acolytes—had of any policy that was instituted by Roosevelt, inspired by idealism, or which involved cooperation with the Soviet Union. The ability of the American conservative establishment to make disreputable what does not serve its interests or beliefs was something that Harry Truman, like many since, did not fully perceive. But for ending the earlier policy—and on this there is now a measure of Soviet agreement—there was no small cooperation from Stalin. And the policy was nailed in its coffin by the Korean War. With others, I think that war was misinterpreted—that the common assumption at the time, that it was a signal of Soviet imperial intentions, was wrong. It was, like much since in that part of the world, a matter of local inspiration. It remains that the North Koreans went to Pusan, and no one could easily imagine they were our clients. Those who argued for working things out with the Soviets were silenced—or committed to saving their skins from Joe McCarthy.

From this point on, the foreign policy of the United States became comprehensively anti-communist. And this anti-communism caused it, in turn, to be increasingly theological, military, bureaucratic and secretive. The theology, of course, was that communism was wicked and, like the devil, relentless. In contrast, free enterprise and democracy—terms liturgically preferable to capitalism—were good but, as with virtue over the ages, beset. With the arrival of John Foster Dulles in 1952, the religious overtones of the policy were formally affirmed. Dulles, we may recall, spoke regularly not of communism but of atheistic communism.

World communism, as the Korean War was thought to show, relied ultimately on military means; it was, accordingly, something to be resisted primarily by armed power—thus the military character of the defense. Liberals, retreating from McCarthy or concerned for their security clearances, could still aver that communism was the consequence of economic deprivation, and that the remedy was social amelioration and economic development. But this, through the fifties and early sixties, was the soft position. The tougher, more practical view was that resistance depended on troops, fire power, nuclear weapons and the associated submarines and missiles. Those who so averred got the good notices from Joseph Alsop.

Since the communist threat was comprehensive— since it discovered and probed points of weakness anywhere in the world, as the Korean experience seemed to show—it had to be comprehensively watched and countered. This required a massive organization. Thus the bureaucratic nature of the policy. The communists operated by conspiracy and stealth. They had to be so countered. This, and the military character of their threat, necessitated the secrecy.

The policy, and its attributes as just adumbrated, largely determined the kind of men who were put in charge as well as the way the policy was conducted. The theological character of the policy required men who were capable of simple, forthright belief—men of dogmatic faith for whom a distinction between good and evil was sufficient. It has been argued in the case of both

Dulles and Rusk, the two Secretaries of State who dominated the two decades of the new policy, that the stern Protestantism of their early origins was reflected in their approach to foreign policy. Perhaps there is something to the point. Be this as it may, both were capable of avowing, without seeming doubt, a sternly canonical view of the unrelieved wickedness of communism, the inherent and even absolute virtue of almost any alternative.

The military character of the policy required men who accepted the use of force, who were untroubled by the vast uncertainties as to outcome whenever there is resort to arms, who were impervious to the moral problems associated with bombing and body counts. The bureaucratic as well as the military character of the policy required men who accepted discipline, operated contentedly within a prescribed formula, understood that you get along by going along, protected their "effectiveness" by controlling carefully their dissent, accepted that, ultimately, the goals of the organization must prevail. This is the ethic of the organization man.

The imperatives of secrecy made winning of support unnecessary. It takes very little persuasive talent to say of an action that it is justified by urgent considerations of national security which cannot be revealed. Secrecy was also essential as a shield for the deeper tendencies of a military and bureaucratic policy. For it is known that these encourage the individual who, however accomplished in bureaucratic survival, is otherwise congenitally incompetent. Secrecy, and the frequently repellent character of the clandestine activities so protected, had a further effect on personnel procurement. It attracted those who, escaping from the confining virtue of civilized existence, rejoiced in what seemed to be a professional license for indecency. Nothing growing out of the Watergate episode has been more salutary than its advertisement of the banality, ineptitude and general unattractiveness of the people who, released from foreign employment, had sought to bring the darker arts, nurtured by our recent foreign policy, to domestic purposes. The demonstration was an accident but it would have been worth arranging.

The old policy propelled us into the Vietnam war, and that was its grave. That this should have happened, given the men that the policy attracted, is not surprising. Those who resolve matters by dogma do not readily reconsider their course. Those whose faith is based on arms do not readily inquire whether soldiers can contend with historical process and revolutionary dynamic. Men skilled in bureaucratic survival do not readily question, or seek to alter, even disastrous bureaucratic purpose. Men accustomed to the protection of secrecy do not have—or else they lose—the capacity to persuade or defend. All who opposed the Vietnam war will agree that nothing was ever so inept as the defense.

The executive and military power did not, nevertheless, readily surrender its commitment to the Indochina involvement. But in what historians will surely concede to be a truly prodigious display of public power, it was eventually forced to do so. We should be proud. Never before has public opinion so asserted itself to halt a war. And with the end to the Indochina involvement has come a drastically reduced view of what we *can* do and what we *need* to do to affect the economic and political development of countries economically, culturally and geographically apart from our own. Complementing the withdrawal from Indochina has come also a revised view of the intentions of the Soviet and Chinese communists. This is a matter on which fairness, however uncomfortable in these matters, requires one to ascribe a strongly affirmative role to the leadership of President Richard Nixon and Secretary Henry Kissinger.

The new policy, if it persists, will attract a better and safer class of men. A policy of détente and accommodation with the communist powers requires men of essentially secular view—men for whom intelligent compromise does not mean surrender to the devil. Additionally, if we recognize that we cannot and that we need not affect the economic and political structure of the countries of the third world, it follows that unilateral military effort in these countries is unnecessary or irrelevant. So military influence on policy is excluded—including the influence not alone of generals but of the civilian Bonapartes whose influence in the last two decades has, if anything, been even more malign. And if we are not reacting to communism in Chad, Angola or Paraguay, we no longer need a vast organization to watch and counter communist machinations, real or imagined. We cannot hope to escape bureaucracy and bureaucrats in this world. They are a part of the genius or non-genius of our age. But in the conduct of foreign policy in the third world its and their role will be less. Specifically there is nothing about this policy in these countries that requires secrecy. If we are not seeking to counter some hidden enemy, we do not need to hide our own work. What we do in the third world can be open and visible and the Congress and the public can rightly ask that it be defended. And our actions will be infinitely safer if they are in the hands of men who must defend what they do.

I've been speaking of the third world—not of Europe, Japan, or the older British Commonwealth. But it was in the third world, let us remind ourselves, that our policy brought us the disasters in these last years. That is because policy in Europe and Japan, where we deal through strong, sophisticated governments, has not lent itself to simple theological decision. In these parts of the world military influence, if present, has not been dominant and the role of bureaucracy—intelligence, clandestine activities, propaganda, military operations—has been far less comprehensive than in the third world. Northern Laos has been a natural theater for the CIA but not northern Alberta or even northern Sweden. Our policy in these parts of the world has not required or attracted the wrong kind of men. It has not, accordingly, reflected their genius for disaster.

A policy that attracts the wrong men has another consequence, including the effect on the way the United States is regarded in the world. The men who were brought into positions of prominence by the creative and compassionate policies of the period of World War II and following kept us out of trouble. (Marshall kept us out of China; the faith that motivated Dulles or Rusk would surely have plunged us in.) Such men, by their caution, imagination and tolerance of differing views caused us also to be well regarded in the world. Men of dogmatic tendency—generals, military or civilian—those who have surrendered to bureaucratic discipline, spies and perpetrators of dirty tricks do not enlist esteem. A policy that nurtures the wrong kind of people also nurtures national disesteem.

Although in foreign policy, as in economics and love, there are few absolutes, the lesson seems plain: men make the policy. But, even more importantly, the policy makes or specifies the men. Henceforth we must be exceedingly suspicious of those policies that get us the wrong kind of men. If there is a hint of simple, dogmatic formula; if there is heavy reliance on military means; if a large organization is required; if secrecy is an imperative; if there can be no defense to the Congress and the public—then our suspicions must be immediately and deeply aroused. Given such policy, the wrong men are inevitable. And whatever the ends to be served, the words of Wellington on seeing his new battalions must be deeply on our minds. The men required by such policy may not frighten the enemy but, by God, they should frighten us.

John Kenneth Galbraith is Paul M. Warburg Professor of Economics at Harvard and former U.S. Ambassador to India.

The Relationship of
Government and Media

James C. Thomson, Jr.

I first got a vivid sense of the government-media relationship, in Washington at least, when as an ambitious youth of twenty-seven I sought, in the late Fifties, the advice of ex-Secretary of State Dean Acheson as to what to be when I grew up. Older men are invariably charmed by such questions from the young since it gives them a chance to talk about themselves, so he graciously gave his answer over martinis and Crab Maryland at the Metropolitan Club. As I was sitting there, exhilarated by the presence of a score of notables among our fellow lunchers, a murmur of excitement filled the room, and two men made their way slowly, in single file, toward a table at the end. From all over came respectful calls of greeting—"Hello there, Scotty!" "Hi, Scotty!" "Good to see you, Scotty!"—to each of which the rather chunky man in front responded, queen-mother-like, with a nod, gentle smile, and slight benediction of the hand. As conversation resumed, my host turned to his friend Paul Nitze at the next table and asked, "Paul, *who* is that with Scotty Reston?" "I don't know," said Nitze, "but I'll certainly find out, and I'll give you a call after lunch."

I should have known then and there where the power really lay—and gone off at once to knock at the door of *The Times.* Instead, I chose to explore for seven years the alleged "corridors of power" at State and the White House—variously observing journalists, obstructing journalists, misleading them, leaking to them, fraternizing with them, conspiring with them, and often cheering them on. And after seven more years out of government, watching the media from the university, I find myself today mysteriously transformed into a Keeper of Journalists at Harvard.

It is, I assume, on the basis of that two-fold experience—as first a government official, and then an academic, who has throughout consorted with the press—that I have been asked to address an important and perennial topic: the government-media relationship in the making of American foreign policy.

A word of caution at the outset: the topic is not only important and perennial, it is also unresolvable. There is no "final solution," thank goodness, to the government-media problem in a democracy; for the continuing tension between these two powerful institutions is a fundamental life-sign—like blood pressure, for instance—within the democratic body politic. I would therefore warn against all proposed "solutions" that put an end to the tension itself. As with blood pressure, the tension can get perilously high and also comatosely low. But in the science of government, unlike medicine, it is a very tough question to judge precisely when danger points are reached; and one should beware of most judges, especially those whose predilections are unstated.

I read the other day, for instance, the recent report of a distinguished Freedom House panel on "The News Media and the Government," in which the first sentence begins, "Relations between the news media and the executive branch of the federal government are deplorable;" and there is immediately a footnoted dissent by panel member Wallace Westfeldt of NBC-TV news. Says Mr. Westfeldt, "I think this characterization is much overdrawn. The condition that exists between the press and the government may be uncomfortable at times for those people who inhabit those institutions. But the result of this condition has been more information to the people about how their government operates and certainly this is not deplorable."

Mr. Westfeldt is probably right. Is it the government-media relationship that produced the Indochina convulsion both abroad and at home, or is it the increasingly indefensible—and therefore largely concealed—policies of the executive branch? Is it the government-media relationship that produced the Watergate convulsion, or is it the publicly indefensible—and therefore heavily concealed—operations of the executive branch? Should we be "deploring" a poisoned relationship, or, instead, poisonous policies and operations?

Now in an ideal society, of course, things would not have come to such a pass—to a point where a handful of journalists in Vietnam in the early Sixties, and two reporters on a gutsy newspaper last year (in both cases with much assistance from others) had to take on their government in order to help the country reverse course. This, I gather, is what the majority of the Freedom House panel means by "deplorable." In an ideal society we should never have had to reach such a stage of mutual discomfort and recrimination.

But the fact is that we did, thanks largely to the government; that some of the press stepped in to do its job; and that, as Mr. Westfeldt says, today more people have more information about how their government operates. And that is certainly *not* deplorable.

Let me now step back for a moment from such cosmic overview judgments and offer a few simple truths about the government-press relationship on the basis of my own personal observation. First and foremost: officials court the press, and the press courts officials; but the courtship is usually doomed—at best a long-term affair, sometimes a one-night stand, but very seldom matrimony.

The difficulty is one of means versus ends. To each, the other is a convenient means, but their ends are usually quite different. The official wants at best to sell an important administration policy, more often to push the case of his faction within the bureaucratic arena, at worst simply to sell himself (to become known, liked, and sought after, as someone "in the know," perhaps with higher political ambitions which the press might eventually assist). The reporter wants at best to ferret out "the truth," more often to get a few more clues on which to hang a somewhat half-baked story under the gun of a deadline, at worst to feel the warm glow of proximity to power (to become known, liked and sought after as someone worth confiding in, perhaps with higher ambitions, etc.).

The crucial social cement is mutual use; also, depending on the nature of the relationship, mutual flattery. Officials use reporters to pass or plant certain messages and thereby win battles. Reporters use officials to ferret out information and thereby get ahead. Officials are flattered by the attentions of some (certainly not all) journalists—mainly those of columnists, editors and publishers. And journalists are flattered by the attention of some (certainly not all) officials—mainly Presidents, cabinet members, some Assistant Secretaries, a very few Ambassadors, and also the bright young men who service The Great. As for true matrimony, it only occurs when officials very occasionally leave government to join the press, much more often when members of the press take on government jobs.

What I have just described is enacted daily, as most Washingtonians know, in *some* federal offices, behind closed doors; on scores of telephone lines, at least prior to Watergate; in assorted Washington clubs every lunchtime; in the more fashionable downtown French restaurants at the same time; and in various unfashionable restaurants further afield if the transaction is particularly serious and the government-press climate particularly tense. It is also enacted at night, as everyone knows, on the greater Washington cocktail and dinner party circuit where one's credentials as an inside-dopester are constantly put to the test.

This relationship, this mutual courtship, is not in itself a bad thing for the nation, though it *can* have bad effects on individual practitioners, within both the government and the media. Like most things, its practice depends on the values of the people involved, and also on the consequences. It's all a bit like what has come to be known in divinity schools as "situation ethics." The Founding Fathers bequeathed us the dual ideal of a somewhat non-acceptable free press and a somewhat more accountable government—both serving, they hoped, the best interests of the electorate. Of course, they foresaw neither the awesome power of the presidency, despite checks and balances, nor the awesome power of instant communication through the electronic media—a power available, it should be added, to both the government and the press.

What remains so far, despite such changes, is a fairly pluralistic press, and their interaction with some other institutions that should not be entirely overlooked—the Congress, the Judiciary, foreign governments, transnational institutions, and the like. And as long as some pluralism still exists in both primary bodies, its existence is sustained and enriched by the process of mutual courtship.

The crucial point to me is the role of the press as a special kind of check or balance: as not merely the fourth estate or fourth branch of government, but rather the opener of closed or clogged communications both within the government and between the government and the public. The first of these functions has been inadequately understood. The executive branch, in both its domestic and foreign realms, is a congeries of individuals, groupings, and agencies. So-called "policy-making" is an ongoing process of argument, negotiation, and even guerrilla warfare within and among competing and changing components—the process of "bureaucratic politics." Within this process, the press performs an invaluable and probably irreplaceable function: the sending of messages back and forth among individuals, factions and agencies, and the alerting of the public to important battles, unresolved issues, not to mention downright skullduggery.

Let me illustrate with only one story. In late 1965, lower-level China-watchers within the State Department became alarmed over certain Pentagon targeting plans for the bombing of North Vietnam. The plans called for strikes against sites so close to the China border that the Chinese might either feel compelled reluctantly to intervene or at least to shoot down some of our off-course aircraft and thereby perhaps trigger a much wider war. These specialists had tried to make their case to the higher-ups, but in vain; the message had not got through to Messrs. Rusk and McNamara, nor to the White House. The worried officials therefore chose to alert Max Frankel of *The Times*, on his daily rounds at State, that things were looking poorly; they did so carefully and obliquely, but they called his attention to some Peking radio broadcasts about the danger of bombing too close to the China border. Mr. Frankel read the stuff, made some other calls, and put three and three together. The result was a front-page *Times* story the next day saying that China specialists in the government were being locked out of Vietnam planning and were alarmed by impending escalation. Mr. McNamara called Mr. Bundy in a fury, Mr. Bundy called some of the rest of us in a fury, and there was much hell to pay. But the upshot was that Messrs. Rusk, McNamara and Bundy called in the China-watching community for a special Saturday morning session, and said that the targeting plans were at once modified as a result of what those China-watchers said. The press, in short, had performed a vital function.

Such things happen constantly—or at least did so in the years I knew best, under Kennedy and Johnson. The press was an invaluable circuit reconnector within government, once circuits were temporarily broken. In a similar vein, an official or an agency might learn that it or he was in danger and did not actually "win" the last policy battle, as had been thought—all thanks to the press as an intermediary for the "losing" side's continued persistence in the ongoing process of bureaucratic politics.

As for the press as an instrument in alerting the public to important battles, unresolved issues, and skullduggery, Indochina and Watergate provide abundant evidence. But little or none of such evidence would have been available to the public except for the tradition and habit of mutual courtship between individual practitioners in two powerful but still pluralistic institutions.

Beyond message-sending, circuit-reconnecting, and alerting, the government-media relationship can be, and often is, a mutually and importantly educational process. Abroad, in foreign postings for both officials and journalists, mutual learning is the name of the game. The best of the foreign service officers and the best of the overseas press corps are fundamentally in the same business. Everyone from ambassador and bureau chief on down is in the business of information-gathering, analysis, and transmission, the one group for a special client called the U.S. Government, the other for the wider public via some wire service or newspaper or TV network. Inevitably they seek out and use each other. A classic example of such harmonious coexistence has been the government-press relationship among Americans in such special outposts as Hong Kong and Moscow. But it also happens all the time elsewhere—in London, Warsaw, Buenos Aires, Nairobi, and New Delhi. As for the places closer to home, the same holds true, though to a lesser degree. Washington officials can and do learn from reporters, as well as vice versa: not merely what your adversaries in some other bureau or department are saying, but sometimes what your higher-ups or juniors are saying, and also what the word is from foreign embassies and from the reporter's paper's sources abroad.

I usually assured myself, in my Washington days, that I learned slightly more from the journalists who took me out to lunch than I gave to them—though sometimes it was a close question; and sometimes I really blew it, though not often enough to get fired. I once tried, for instance, as a junior flunkey at State in 1961 or 1962, to "humanize" Mr. Rusk's image, which was then quite chilly, by confiding to a newsmagazine friend that on the morning after a certain general had told a congressional committee that the State Department was full of "commies," beginning at the top, Rusk had walked into his staff meeting, shuffled his papers, peered over his glasses and said, with an impish smirk, "Good morning—eh—Comrades!" Well, there was hell to pay for that one, too; and also many new pledges to protect the sanctity of the Secretary's staff meeting. Anyway, my friend got himself an item; but even so I learned from *him* at the same lunch things about Vietnam or the Dominican Republic—I forget which—that my cables hadn't told me. So it was still a reasonably good trade-off.

The fact of the matter is not quite what Chairman Khrushchev said to Allen Dulles, "We employ the same spies, so why don't we get together and pay them one joint fee?" It is rather that reporters and editors working for the press, and reporters and officials working for the various divisions of the government, are all—at their best—poring over the same material. So why not expect, tolerate, and even encourage a certain amount of collusion, as well as healthy competition? But, of course, what gets fed into the government by its reporter-officials does not necessarily see the light of day, much less the eyes of those who count; indeed it is usually "classified," unlike what is sent to newspapers and TV stations—which also may not see the light of day—but usually for less immediately iniquitous reasons—like lack of space and time, or worse, bad executive judgment.

This brings me to another quite obvious point. As bad as the media may be—and they vary from fair to horrendous—their instinct for concealing significant information in foreign affairs is nothing quite like that of the government. To put the matter simply: the system of security classification within the executive branch is a prime cause of our present afflictions. Here I deal with what is now well understood, thanks largely to the Ellsberg case and sundry expert testimony brought to bear upon it: namely, that our security classification system is very largely an absurdity.

I first perceived the point when I found myself in the vestibule of the office of the Under-Secretary of State in early 1961, sorting rather desperately each day through a foot and a half of the most highly classified cables, incoming and outgoing, that had filtered up to that stratosphere. I had to write a memo or two myself, and realizing that everything else in the room bore a classification, sought guidance from my colleague at the next desk. Should what I wrote be classified too, and if so, on what basis? His answer was the time-honored one within the bureaucracy, "Anything you don't want to see on the front page of *The New York Times* tomorrow you should classify." I understood the message. The archives will show, in twenty-five years or so, when they are finally opened to researchers, that all sorts of trivia that emerged from my typewriter bore such stamps as CONFIDENTIAL, SECRET, TOP SECRET, EYES ONLY, LIMIDIS, EXDIS, and even NODIS. I also learned to use the outgoing designation NIACT, which meant that the recipient ambassador should be roused out of bed to reply even if the cable arrived during the night. I should add that in later years some of us thought up the further designation DAYACT, which meant that the ambassador should be roused out of bed to reply even if the cable arrived during the day.

The serious point about classification is, of course, that every administration since World War II has increasingly abused a system whose original rationale was the concealment of national defense information from The Enemy abroad. Concealment from that enemy has receded as a rationale, except for hard-core stuff like troop movements, nuclear weapons information, intelligence relating to codes and the breaking of codes, and the intricacies of any particular delicate international negotiation. Instead, most of what is concealed through classification is anything and everything whose revelation might be politically embarrassing to the administration in power, or to individual officials, in terms of The Enemy at home: the opposition party, the Congress, the press, and thereby the wider voting public. When my friend at the next desk at State talked about not having things appear on the front page of *The Times*, he wasn't talking about the Russians or the Chinese or Hanoi; he was talking about protecting my boss and the President and me from wider *American* scrutiny.

Now privacy is one thing; it has its place in the media as well as in the government. But the use of security classifications for personal and political concealment in the politics of foreign policy-making is an abuse that must somehow be halted. How to do so is a tough question; but one initial step may be, as some have suggested, to hold an official responsible for the classification he gives to a document and to administer penalties for over-classification.

So much for some simple truths. At their heart is an undeniable fact: the existence of a free, probing, and skeptical press is a major obstacle to efficient governance by the executive, to the making of tidy policy, whether foreign or domestic. But then so is the existence of a Congress, an opposition party, and regularly scheduled elections. These are all considerable prices to pay; most societies in the world have found ways to avoid paying them—China, Russia, Greece and now the Philippines, to name only a few. But as long as we still believe in the fallibility of all men and institutions, and as long as we still value the disorder of relative liberty over the efficiency of tyranny, we should probably continue to pay such prices.

One hears a great deal these days about the startling loss of credibility of both government and the media. This, says the Freedom House report, is deeply alarming; among its panelists, one finds no dissenter. But I wonder if things are as bad as they seem; or rather, I wonder if this mutual loss of credibility—confirmed by all sorts of surveys—is really a sign of sickness rather than a necessary stage on the road to national health.

We commemorate this year the twenty-fifth anniversary of a beginning of the Cold War with the Czechoslovak *coup*. We have also celebrated, in the past year or two, beginning of the end of the Cold War, with the Nixon overtures to China and the Soviet Union, and our ending of the Indochina war, or at least our dumping of it. Governments, however, do not turn around without paying a price for their about-face; neither do the institutions that consort with governments—notably the press.

The problem with which we have all been groping is, I think, the problem of the "national security ethic:" the conviction that Presidents-know-best in matters of foreign policy, and that anything goes in the preservation of "national security." We were almost all of us believers (those of us old enough to remember) in the days of Stalin. The Presidency, the military, the bureaucracy, the Congress, the academy, the professions (including the press) were most of them faithful servants of a national security apparatus created to hold the enemy at bay.

But then times changed, and so did perceptions. And like any state cult, the national security ethic developed doubters and even heretics. I.F. Stone was an early one, a pariah in those haunted Fifties; but eventually came younger journalists who broke with the creed, who saw for instance the Vietnam war as something other than Thermopylae. And the consensus itself began to crack; for the enemy was no longer Stalin or even necessarily communism, but rather oppression, hunger, poverty, racism, and many other things. Meanwhile, however, the national security state had focused, from its earliest days, on the enemy within as well as the enemy without—under Democrats as well as Republicans. And although the external enemy went the way of the Cold War, the internal enemy remained, as did the increasingly sophisticated techniques to subdue him.

It is only poetic justice that the Indochina war, which toppled one presidency, is now followed by Watergate, which will cripple, if not topple, another. For as Indochina was the logical consequence of an obsessive and uninformed focus on the enemy without, so Watergate is the logical consequence of an obsessive and uninformed focus on the enemy within.

In both operations—the making of Indochina and Watergate—the press has been somewhat complicitous, because press people, like the rest of us, love their country, like to believe the best of it, and became for a while willing adherents to the national security ethic. But in both operations the press has also played a central role in calling a halt, because press people, at their ornery best, are still eventually skeptical of all ideologies, including that of the national security state.

We *are* in a time of travail for both government and the media—no question. Each institution is certainly under fire—part of our national withdrawal symptoms as we pull out of the Cold War era. But that in itself should cause no great alarm. If one or the other institution were to prevail or to expire, *that* would be cause for alarm. But no such thing is happening. Presidential assistants may eventually go to jail. So, for very different kinds of reasons, may reporters, editors, or publishers. But government and the media are still both very much alive and also kicking. And so, as a result, is the nation.

James C. Thomson, Jr., is Curator, Nieman Fellowships for Journalism, Harvard University, and former Special Assistant to the Secretary of State.

IV

FOREIGN POLICY AND THE MEDIA: THE JOURNALISTS' CRITIQUE

Here the theses advanced by Messrs. Galbraith and Thomson are subjected to comment, analysis and criticism by a panel of journalists, experts on journalism and students of government and foreign policy. There is both agreement and disagreement among them, and Galbraith and Thomson come back for a last word.

Not surprisingly, the journalists on the panel think there is too much secrecy in government, and, not surprisingly, the Nixon Administration doesn't come off very well. However, the journalists are also critical of the media. David Halberstam, author of The Best *and the* Brightest, *feels that in some ways the newspapers are now repeating some of the same mistakes they made before. and Alfred Balk, editor of* Atlas World Press Review, *calls on the media to stop treating itself as "the most sacred cow of all."*

The discussion opens with remarks from John Cogley, editor of The Center Magazine, *who holds "there is a kind of constitutional obligation on the part of the press to do its thing, come hell or high water."*

John Cogley:

The general title of this session, "The Relationship of Government and Media," really amounts to a clarion call for truisms. Of course, if the clichés do not become quite evident in the course of our discussion, it will be probably due to the fact that most of our panelists are journalists and all of them are professional word wizards. They have learned from experience or are natively endowed with the ability to make an old truth sound like a brilliant new insight. That is quite the contrary, I might add, of the run-of-the-mill academics, who sometimes seem to specialize in making fresh insights sound like tired platitudes. Now, a notable exception, of course, is Kenneth Galbraith. He is part journalist, part academic, which gives him a kind of double competence that puts him out front in both groups. I suppose this also gets him in difficulties with both groups. Some think he is too entertaining to be taken seriously in the Academy, and others hold he is too insightful to belong among the "mere journalists." Mr. Galbraith deals in clichés only in the sense that he originally mints them as shiny new coins; but his influence is so vast that a Galbraithian insight soon enough becomes a journalists' cliché.

We may be doomed to truisms in this discussion for a good reason: the issues to which we are addressing ourselves were long ago settled in the United States, at least at a theoretical level. There is nothing we are likely to say, no matter how well we say it, that will improve upon the First Amendment.

A sage once said about the whole body of philosophic literature, "After Plato, everything else is commentary." After the First Amendment, in this connection, everything else is commentary. But the commentary has to be made, and it has to be made again and made still once again, because the freedom of the press is like the virtue of the innocent: it is constantly being threatened. Journalists know however that if they ever succumb they will have betrayed their profession and not only their profession but themselves and the nation itself.

The word "betrayed" here is not too strong, I think. We don't swear in newspaper people or TV commentators with an oath of office or hold them under threat of impeachment, but maybe it would not be too bad an idea if we found some way of doing so. The fact is that there is a kind of constitutional obligation on the part of the press to do its thing, come hell or high water. And its thing is simply to tell the truth, the whole truth, and nothing but the truth. Of course there are always good solid reasons offered as to why it will serve the nation, benefit the common good, or better mankind itself if we settle for something less than the truth, the whole truth, and nothing but the truth. The proposals will amount to seemingly harmless, and sometimes even rather noble-sounding propositions, like appeals to patriotism: don't report plans for the Bay of Pigs invasion, for example, because it will endanger the operation; don't probe too deeply, or probe at all, into CIA operations, you might endanger national security, etc.

No one ever says baldly, just forget about your solemn obligation to deal with the truth, tell a few fibs or hold back some important truth because it will make life easier for us. The stated objective is almost always replete with moral precepts about higher duties and greater claims. What we are urged to do is not to tell lies as such but to shade the truth in behalf of the uppercase Truth. Every scoundrel in history perhaps has lied in behalf of the Truth. Journalists are sometimes tricked into the same fallacy by appeals to their better nature, probably at least as often as they are misled by their acquisitive instincts.

I would not deny that there are genuine problems. For instance, one wouldn't lightly report on a troop movement in wartime. But I believe that these special occasions are much rarer than we are usually led to believe. If there is a general rule I think it might go something like this: newspeople not only have a right, they have a duty to inform the People—the capital "P" People, who are the ultimate rulers of the nation—of whatever the People have a right to know, and not only a right to know, but a need to know if they are going to continue their experiment with self-government. And that is almost always a great deal more than the elected leaders usually think the People have a right or a need to know. The conscientious journalist, then, is not a "mere" anything. He or she, in a very real sense, is as much of a representative of the people as those who sit in the halls of Congress or in the Oval Office at the White House.

Who elected Walter Cronkite? We heard that a few years ago. I think that Mr. Cronkite is re-elected every evening, every time millions of Americans turn on their TV sets. When they decide to throw him out of office, they will no longer switch on that particular channel. That means that not only Walter Cronkite but the lowliest reporter of the smallest newspaper is burdened with a terrible responsibility, duty, and obligation. This is what we want to talk about.

John Cogley is a Senior Fellow of the Center for the Study of Democratic Institutions and Editor, The Center Magazine.

Peter Irvin Lisagor:

Mr. Galbraith may be one of the few men in the world who suffers from a myopia of hindsight. I had thought that the policy of détente commended itself, at least tentatively, until I heard the good professor embrace it as a faith that was embraceable for at least twenty-five years. I suspect the policy may survive his endorsement. My problem with Jim Thomson's paper is that I agree with much of it. That troubles me. I should be jumping on his neck for even suggesting a faintly incestuous relationship between the government and the media. In keeping with our two-fisted, romantic tradition, the answer to this mutual courtship business should be, "We wouldn't touch it with a ten-foot pole!" In the field of foreign policy, alas, there is hanky-panky. It is no more pronounced today, however, than in the field of health, education and welfare or defense or justice or other specialized areas. But I suspect that a reporter gets more mileage out of remarking casually, "As I was saying to Henry just the other day . . . " than he would in disclosing a familiarity with the heads of other departments. Still, it is a violation of the arm's length principle which ought to guide the hardnosed professional.

Jim Thomson speaks of his time in Washington during the 1960s when a certain civility governed the government-media relationship. As one who goes back to the Administration of Rutherford B. Hays, I, too, can remember when there were said to be three foreign offices in Washington, one at *The New York Times,* one at the *Washington Post*, and, last and least, the State Department. What James Reston, Walter Lippmann, the Alsop brothers, and other thunderbolt-hurlers of the time were saying about foreign policy mattered greatly. It often got cranked into foreign policy formulations. Their critiques were important, and they were indispensable in the merchandising of policy. In the Washington of

Richard Nixon, however, at least up to this point, we haven't had to worry about such things as courtships. In an inspired moment the journalist William Manchester described Lyndon Johnson as a man who believed the shortest distance between two points was through a tunnel. A dyspeptic critic of President Nixon might say that he believed the shortest distance between two points is through a tunnel sealed at both ends. And Henry Kissinger, whose gifts include a considerable skill at giving newsmen a soothing eucalyptus rub when required, made secrecy sound like a patriotic virtue.

It is my view that the secrecy, much of it, was more a reflection of the President's personal secretiveness than any imperative of anybody's policy. The entry into China, to cite an example, need not have been all that surreptitious, as Senator Sam Ervin would like to say. In fact, a few discreet smoke signals might have spared us the problem with Japan.

Let me say that I believe this problem of the government and media has been analyzed to the point that we've come to believe that there are structural defects in it. Or, to maintain Jim Thomson's metaphor, the tendency is to conclude that they are institutionally incompatible and hence require unseemly chaperones in the form of court decisions bearing on the First Amendment and its relationship to the Sixth Amendment. There seems to be a compulsive need to come up with novel analyses of what's wrong with the relationship. This leads often to a distortion or an exaggeration of the problem. The Nixon Administration, or more accurately the White House, or part of it, has tried to portray the press as a hostile force, an alien element, somehow separated from the public interest. Well, if we don't represent the public interest we really don't represent anything. The press is not a corporate entity with one head and employees who behave with cookie-cutter conformity. The wholesome competitiveness provides self correction. Flagrant errors or abuses are quickly spotlighted and just as quickly condemned. There are imperfections, to be sure, too many of them. But with a high degree of professionalism and a healthy measure of skepticism about the work of all governments, the media is less likely to do the Republic in than those who are uneasy with power and have no decent respect for its limits.

Peter Irvin Lisagor is Chief, Washington Bureau, Chicago Daily News.

Alfred Balk :

Mr. Galbraith stressed that we require in government men of a secular view. I would say in the press that at minimum we certainly must have some agnostics. Regarding Jim Thomson's point about Scotty Reston and where the power really lies, I would like to quote David Brinkley on being careful not to overestimate his power. Brinkley said, "Remember, no press ever overthrew a government." I know Jim was merely setting the scene, but let us beware of overestimating the power of even big media such as the electronic networks.

As Governor Rockefeller said, telecommunications, the computer and information technology have launched us on a social revolution of historic magnitude, and we have only begun to consider its implications. One implication is the indispensability of sophisticated journalism that can impart perspective to the onset of change—a future shock change of pace—and its demands upon us, including the foreign policy imperatives for governments. Only to the extent that we have that kind of sophisticated journalism are we likely to have an open and enlightened foreign policy. I urge those seeking to shape foreign policy along the lines of humaneness and reason not to lose sight of the indispensability of an improved press, of a quality press (and I include broadcasting). I say this because the press must remain free, which means it must be credible and trusted. I suggest that in the future it should be *instantly* trusted, or recognizable as trustworthy, in any confrontation with big government. As the power of telecommunications and the capacity to manipulate the channels of communication by government increase, this may become imperative. We must at least have instant skepticism, we in the public and in the press.

We should know now, I think, that the First Amendment is only what the courts say it is, that "commentary" is still going on, and appointees to the courts do reflect the political climate. And the press must be concerned about public attitudes toward it, about public trust in it. Now this means that the owners of American news media, along with all of us for whom they hold First Amendment rights in trust, must ask some hard questions. For example, even though corporate news media must earn a profit, should they, as now, be among the select few most lucrative industries in the nation? *Excessive profits earned at the expense of journalistic quality constitute a national scandal which cries for public airing.*

There are other questions, and these apply directly to foreign affairs. American journalism has improved, but its definition of news is outmoded. It is still better at exposing than explaining. Its training and staffing are inadequate. It is mainly white, male, upper and middle-class oriented. It's reluctant to acknowledge and correct errors. And despite fulminations to the contrary, it is predominantly a one-party press—Republican, albeit independent Republican. These are conditions that I think challenge universities, foundations, citizen groups and working journalists who must be creative catalysts to bring change.

A modest first goal surely would be to stimulate regular, serious, analytical coverage of the media's most sacred cow of all—the media. That's not easy, believe it or not. It also means experimenting with things like journalism reviews, which on the local level are beginning to spring up, to monitor, to write about what's in the press of a region or a locality. We should experiment also with lay-and-journalist media councils to form a liaison between the public and the press and to monitor and analyze the media. And we need convocations like this which can carry on a dialogue about government and the media.

There also should be more alternative media, especially that fourth network of public television whose funding still is precarious. All of you ought to be making noises about that. If we have only three nationwide networks we're undernourished. We simply must have more channels, especially for serious programming. Most of all, we as citizens of this democracy must do our homework. Democracy is a complicated and, some say, a messy way of governing human affairs. As the Director General of the BBC told me recently in an interview, things are never simple. We must remember that when talking about government and the media.

Let me cite examples. Take the issue of confidential sources. I recently fought a case to the Supreme Court on this issue, involving my right to keep the source of a magazine article confidential, and I won. Washington newsmen have fought similar battles. These are all for good reason and I'm afraid that many of our friends in the bar and many laymen don't understand what's involved. We simply can't get sensitive information unless we are assured we can keep the source confidential. Remember, Truth is elusive; it must emerge from a multitude of voices. We must have that multitude of voices and we must be able to keep confidential sources confidential.

Take also the matter of news leaks. Spiro Agnew made a cause celebre of this. Incidentally, I wonder if any of you have considered the irony of how the announcement of Agnew's resignation came? I'm told

that an Associated Press newsman, upon hearing that
Agnew was in Baltimore, called Agnew's office in
Washington, and asked for Marsh Thompson, his press
secretary. Thompson's secretary answered the phone and
said, "Oh, Mr. Thompson can't talk to you, the Vice-
President has resigned." An inadvertent news leak, of all
things, in that place! One person's news leak, we must
always remember, is another person's parting of a curtain
so that the people may see.

So when the rhetoric heats up I would counsel: let
us keep cool heads about press-and-government issues. All
of our institutions are interdependent, all must be
humanized and made responsive to future shock and its
demands upon us. This is a time of confusion. I say to
both government and the press, let us get on with the
humanizing and with the reforming, in deed as well as in
words.

Alfred Balk is Editor of Atlas World Press Review *and former
Editor of the* Columbia Journalism Review.

Thomas E. Cronin:

The two gentlemen from Harvard have essentially given
us a message which can be summed up in these
observations: first, making the presidency safe for democracy is a proposition whose time has come; second, the
tragedy of the Sixties, and the recent period as well, has
been that being President regrettably means never having
to say you're sorry—or wrong.

I am sufficiently persuaded by the good man theory,
or the good person theory, put forward by Mr. Galbraith,
and also the analysis of the problems of government and
media put forward by Mr. Thomson and his men, that
sunlight is the best of disinfectants in a society such as
ours that I suggest that we ought to nominate
Mr. Galbraith as Vice-President and Mr. Thomson as his
press secretary.

I am troubled a bit, however, with both papers. I would like to add a few observations of my own. The "good person" theory put forward by Mr. Galbraith reminds me of the complaint frequently heard by those who specialize in the area of corrections and rehabilitation in prison reform. They frequently suggest that it would be very helpful to them if they just had a better class of prisoners. Now, as an aside, I would suggest that Mr. Nixon perhaps is contributing some solution to their problems by sending the members of the press or members of his own Administration to the prisons. But I would submit also that the good man theory, or the good person theory alone is not enough. It's not a sufficient response, I think, to the problems we face today. We must, I think, concern ourselves also with organizational problems, which though they may be subordinate to a good man and good people staffing the top echelons in government, are also critically important.

I think I am in agreement, by and large, with what Mr. Thomson said. The relationship between the media and the President is, and will continue to be, one of mutual manipulation. The President will always, regardless of who he is, want cheerleaders among the press corps. How to look presidential without being President frequently is the code and the script for the public relations staff at the White House. One of the most disconcerting, disquieting developments of the past decade has been precisely the vast swelling of the presidency in the area of its public relations machine. In the same way that Mr. Clark Clifford called for lowering the defense budget, I would suggest we insist that Congress cut the public relations budget of the White House in half.

Now for a few propositions I'd like to submit for your consideration. The slogan, or cliché that what is advantageous for the presidency is necessarily good for the nation, is one whose time has passed. We need a healthy skepticism toward what any President says on any subject. What is good for the President is not necessarily good for the nation.

There is a second proposition that needs to be carefully examined. The public administration professionals—ever since the Roosevelt Administration—have been suggesting, if not shouting, that the President needs help. I would suggest that the President right now does need help, but that it need not take the form of a larger and larger staff surrounding the executive office, overburdening it, overspecializing it, overcompartmentalizing it. This large staff is almost crushing the presidency by sheer weight, so much so that it is not able to listen to Congress or listen to the American people, but mainly listens only to itself.

A third proposition is that when an ordinary citizen somehow gets elevated to the presidency, he becomes ennobled, uplifted, strengthened, and his sense of history somehow enables him to behave with much higher standards and sense of purpose and sense of respect and dignity than otherwise would be the case. I call this proposition into question, and even suggest that in the past two presidencies at least, the reverse may well have been the case. That proposition needs serious attention; certainly it should not be perpetuated by either the press or the political scientists.

As we now look to the 1976 elections, or the replacement of a President by other means, we can no longer afford to tolerate the notion that we can separate politics and the presidency. We have not suffered by too much politics in the presidency; we have suffered because Richard Nixon has not been an open, democratic, political leader. He has been a covert leader who has tried to be popular and to do what is popular and to make his reputation for the future, but he has ducked and ducked, time and again, the responsibilities of the truly democratic political personage in this country. We can no more take the politics out of the presidency than we can take the presidency out of politics. Furthermore it is not desirable to take the politics out of the presidency. The important thing is to have a healthy, constructive, open sense of politics, a politics that listens, a politics that consults the people and consults the Congress.

When a president of the United States tries to be above politics, what results generally is that he and his aides grow dependent on a more secretive and covert political operation. This has long been the case, but it's far more so in the recent months. The convenience of secrecy and the cloak of national security justifications are extraordinarily tempting to those who want to avoid appearing to be partisan political leaders. Such secrecy, however, invariably conceals mistakes, deviousness, capriciousness, and, as we now know, illegalities of vast proportions. The attempted divorce, I submit, between the presidency and politics presupposes a significantly different political system than ours or than the one which we want in this country. In light of the requisites of democracy, the presidency must be a highly open, as well as a highly political office. And the President must be an expert practitioner of the art of making the difficult and desirable possible. Quite simply, there is no other way for presidents to accomplish what is so badly needed to be accomplished. The President who remains aloof from politics, from campaigns, who tries to contract out his re-election campaign, who tries to avoid being associated with his national political party, who foregoes lending his assistance to political members in his own party, who dismantles and ignores his national party, as both Presidents Johnson and Nixon have done, does so at the risk of becoming a prisoner of events, special interests, and his own whims. And this indeed is what we have seen.

And as far as bipartisanship is concerned, James MacGregor Burns put it very aptly when he said, "Almost as many crimes have been committed in the name of mindless bipartisanship as in the name of mindless patriotism."

Thomas E. Cronin was a Visiting Fellow of the Center, and former Research Political Scientist at The Brookings Institution.

David Halberstam:

There is a tendency when people in the press and people who believe in a free press get together on an occasion like this to emphasize the sins of the government, to talk about how we are manipulated, how we are used, the threats to our liberties, etc. I've really come here to say that I think the faults are largely our own, our own failings, our own sins. That term "news management" is a foolish phrase. Sure, there is news management and sure, the government spends a lot paying Assistant Secretaries of State for public affairs, and Assistant Secretaries of Defense for public affairs—twenty-five or thirty or thirty-five thousand dollars a year. We should not be surprised. The real news managers, it seems to me, are the managing editors and editors of the various newspapers, the bureau chiefs, and others who do not insist on a special kind of integrity within their bureaus, particularly here in Washington, which I think has perhaps the most corrupt journalistic practices anywhere in the country. These news managers do not insist upon individual integrity on the part of their reporters, do not set a tonal quality of adversary relationship and, above all, do not give their reporters enough time and space to do the really contrary and adversary reporting that is needed. I think the failings are our own. I think we are, indeed, very free, but we do not use our freedoms enough. I think we accommodate to power, and we have done so for far too long.

Ken Galbraith outlined the Cold War, and how foreign policy became centrist, consensus-oriented. What he really didn't go into at any great length is the way the press itself willingly acquiesced for so long, be it Vietnam or Watergate. There is now the great moment of triumph—how well the press has behaved! It really hasn't behaved so well. Washington journalism, all throughout Vietnam, largely accommodated to the mores of the government; and throughout Watergate, until the very last, when McCord began to babble a little bit. All but a very few reporters went the other way. Those who by reason of their power, prestige, resources had the opportunities, were the least active. Who really fought the battle? A couple of young reporters, not the power and the might and majesty of the Washington journalistic establishment. And it was the same in regard to Vietnam.

There is an accommodation to power. Reporters too often become an extension of the institution they cover. They begin indeed to represent it. It is an insidious thing, a subtle thing. It's the same kind of thing you get in the sports department when you assign a reporter to a baseball team, and, after awhile, he doesn't want to face the people the next day if he has written critically. So he doesn't really tell you the negative stuff. He no longer serves the public interest of the reader. He serves his own interest and his own "cronyism" in what he is covering. The reporter takes on the coloration of the institution and begins to represent it.

A classic example in Washington reporting of the kind of thing I am talking about took place during the Vietnam war when reporters for *Time* and *Newsweek* out in Vietnam would again and again file tough-minded, critical reports from the field. Their colleagues here in Washington, covering State and Defense, would undermine them and file positive, government-oriented reporting. And then the hamburger machines of *Time* and *Newsweek* would immediately dilute the freshness and the toughness of mind coming out of Saigon. These are failings within our own profession, very much.

I think that one of the problems is the institutional norm of our profession. Reporters who take on the main institutions, the government, can do it once. But if you do it twice, you become a little controversial and a little kinky and no longer quite respectable. And so the kind of people who rise within the journalistic institutions themselves are the people who are talented, bright, but by and large have never really been themselves in an adversary relationship; they have never gone into the pit. I'd be hard put, thinking of American journalism, and people at the lever of power in American journalism, to name anybody who had really gone into the pit or had any kind of serious adversary relationship with the government of the United States. Not the government of Poland, like Abe Rosenthal in *The New York Times*, but the government of the United States of America. And don't tell me there is not infinite corruption and scandal and abuse of power that over thirty years make reputations and project men, not just to write a column, the way Tom Wicker and Tony Lewis do, but to the levers of power. There's a very important difference.

One of the things that has always struck me—I guess you could call it Halberstam's Law—is that journalistic capacity to be different or better or really critical of the institutions you cover is in inverse proportion to the power of your platform. I suppose that's why you have had Izzy Stone, so critical and so brilliant during the years of the Vietnam war, while the main news commentators on the networks and the White House correspondents for the great newspapers were so pallid. I think a codicil of Halberstam's Law is that the fancier the restaurant, and the fancier the dinner party in Washington, and the higher the official who attends with the journalist, the less likely the public interest is going to be served and the more likely the state and the governmental institution is going to be served. As a corollary to that, the smaller the restaurant, the darker the corridor, and the lower the government official, the better you are going to be served.

Do not think for a moment that the Pentagon Papers was a great victory for the press. It was indeed a scandal. It underlined what the press itself had not done, which was seriously to go into any kind of analysis of how and why we had gone wrong in Vietnam. I myself am grateful for that, because I was working on a book at the time, and I could have been knocked out by these newspapers and magazines which had vaster resources taking up the subject. Instead, it became a story when they got the documents. Now, if it was worth sixty pages in *The New York Times* and the Washington *Post*, why didn't some managing editor assign it? The Pentagon Papers is indeed a judgment, not just against a bureaucracy which lied and manipulated, but it is a judgment, if you read it carefully, against the press corps which allowed itself to be manipulated. Again and again in there you will find what the intelligence people were really saying out of Saigon. And you would find also that the White House would call in the great Washington reporters and say, "Our intelligence says—" which, of course, was not what the intelligence people were saying. And the White House reporters would write, "White House intelligence says," instead of "The White House claims that its intelligence says."

And so what happens after the Pentagon Papers come out? The very institutions that congratulate themselves go right back to doing the same thing. In May, 1972, at the time of the spring offensive of the North Vietnamese, the major bureau chiefs went right back to Kissinger, and Kissinger once again said, "Our intelligence sources say," and they put it down just the same way, when indeed the CIA and "pure intelligence" over many years were much more critical. But the manipulated press went along. The way indeed the press went along with Kissinger, the man who is a known prevaricator and wire-tapper. The degree to which the Washington press corps played his game is a textbook example of manipulation. Dear Lord, he was good at it! You know, you could come down to the city and hear people say, "I just saw Henry." It made you want to retch, because anybody who saw Henry was seeing Henry on Henry's terms.

So I leave you with these happy thoughts. There is no lack of freedom in this country. Anybody who has ever been a correspondent in Eastern Europe, as I have, and comes back here, indeed comes back with a sadness, because we have the freedoms and they do not. But we use perilously few of them.

David Halberstam is author of The Best and The Brightest *and former* New York Times *foreign correspondent.*

Richard Holbrooke:

After Dave Halberstam's ringing defense of his colleagues in the press, I guess I'm here to defend the United States government, of which I was formerly and still am, half a part. Before I get to Jim Thomson's paper, I would like to make a brief point on Mr. Galbraith's paper. I don't agree with it. I don't think men are attracted to Washington by the substance of policy. On the contrary, I think they're attracted by the power that the city offers them. Power, not the substance of policy, brings men here. As Stanley Karnow of *The New Republic* has said, observing people who have wanted to come to this city from places such as New York, Cambridge and elsewhere, most of them would work for any man in the Oval Office just for the chance to have part of the action. And that's also true of most civil servants.

Jim Thomson opened his speech with a wonderful story which conveys I think almost everything one would want to convey about the relationship between the government and the press in this city. Except perhaps the sequel to the story. Now, I wasn't there and neither was

Jim, but one can construct what the Pentagon would call a logical scenario for what happened after that lunch. Paul Nitze probably did some checking around with friends and found out that the man Scotty Reston was lunching with was a minor bank official, let's say, from the Midwest. What Mr. Nitze did not find out was that he was really the second cousin of Mrs. Reston. And that was the only reason they were lunching at the Metropolitan Club. But, no matter. Via the usual channels, Reston's wife's second cousin's name was the talk of the dinner party circuit within three days in Washington. Washington loves to talk about names. Here's a new one: hearing that Reston is lunching with an unknown financier from the American heartland, one of the Alsop brothers and Roland Evans each decide they must beat James Reston to the story. And they vie for the honor of taking him to the Metropolitan Club themselves. After several more lunches in those restaurants that Dave Halberstam talked about, the Midwest banker finds himself an item in the Washington *Post's* social columns. Shortly therafter his name is mentioned by William White and Drew Pearson as a possible Secretary of the Treasury. A few weeks later, to no one's great surprise, save maybe Reston's, he's named a member of the Securities and Exchange Commission.

Beyond that addendum to Jim Thomson's message, it's hard to add much to his brilliant and candid exposition of the odd love-hate relationship between journalists and officials. They use each other. It is as simple, as brutal, and as self-serving as that. When I entered the State Department in 1963, it amazed me to find how great the hostility was to journalists on the part of many government officials. I had thought that it was a legitimate part of a reporter's job to try to get information, that it was a legitimate part of a government official's job to give him anything to which any ordinary American citizen was entitled. I'd like to emphasize that point. I don't believe that the reporter deserves special treatment. If somebody comes in off the street who is not a reporter and asks a question, the same question as a reporter, he should get the same answer. After all, I thought then, we're a democracy and the government owes the people an explanation of its action. I could see many circumstances in which the press and the government would have different objectives or different interests, as Jim Thomson points out. But this seemed a legitimate part of the game. The press had its role and we had ours.

Then my first assignment was Vietnam, and things turned out very differently. I was warned almost instantly about the press. You can't trust any of them. And about the same time I was introduced through a mutual friend to the man most dangerous to American policy objectives in Indochina, David Halberstam of *The New York Times.* The problem became personal and not at all theoretical. I liked Halberstam and thought he was doing a good job. Even when I disagreed with him I could not understand why he and his colleagues were being accused often of being traitors by senior government officials. Had we forgotten in the government that the professional relationship between the government and the press simply had to be adversarial? One could easily understand the annoyance of people in the government at some of Halberstam's stories and stories of those of his colleagues like Neil Sheehan, but not the accusations of treason or anti-Americanism. Yet I heard these made.

As the war went on, and as the gap between official rhetoric and newspaper reporting grew, the cries that reporters were un-American also grew. Only a few officials were stupid enough to make the accusations publicly, but they were heard often, obsessively, in private. Some officials, in fact, were extremely polite to reporters, some officials were even good sources to reporters, but they would outdo each other in the privacy of the Embassy in denouncing the latest stab in the back by the press. I'm not going to dwell on the accuracy of the reporting from Saigon. Some reporters were good, some were terrible. My point simply is that they were not un-American. They were reporters and were never asked to take an oath to the government. They never were paid by the U.S. government. They were not part of the big U.S. government machine. They had a different job to do, and it was a legitimate job. The same, of course, applies to other great confrontations between press and the government, including Watergate and the Agnew affair.

This distrust of the press is based on several deep-seated factors. Let me mention but two. First of all, there's the tremendous risk to one's career in the government if one is visibly identified as a friend of journalists. A simple-minded syllogism is widely believed in Washington, especially by high level officials who, ironically, are often themselves the source of the major leaks. The syllogism: (1) a man knows journalists; (2) he therefore must be giving them information; (3) giving information to journalists is, by definition, leaking; (4) leaking is bad; (5) a man who knows journalists, therefore, is doing something bad. As a result, his career is often at great risk, he may suffer badly. The consequences are clear. A career in the government is one in which you openly show your hostility to the press, or at least your total lack of association with them. It can't hurt within the government, and maybe by your very hostility you will show up the supposed weakness of other people who know journalists. In furtherance of this axiom, I have even seen government officials be rude to reporters at parties in front of fellow government workers and be reasonably pleasant to the same reporters when they think no one is looking.

A second and more basic point: We are aware that in the last eight or nine years the battle between the government and the press has brought into our vocabulary the phrase "credibility gap." By this is meant a deliberate attempt on the part of the government to lie to the people. But this obscures a more fundamental point. Why do Presidents and other politicians and bureaucrats lie? I think lying must be understood here as the front edge, the public front edge, of a much larger failure, a failure on the part of some of our leaders to believe in and live by the democratic principles on which our nation is supposedly based. The evidence suggests to me the gloomy conclusion that our government leaders lie publicly because they're acting in an anti-democratic manner privately.

I would view the credibility gap, then, in a somewhat different way. The government has lost the confidence of the American people because it lies, it lies because it has lost confidence in the values of a genuinely open and democratic society. Secrecy is the inevitable first step in such a process. Lying under pressure and probing from outsiders—good journalists, good Congressmen—is inevitably the next step. Thus the circle is joined, and the circle, of course, is a vicious one.

Such events as Watergate have done much to bring the press back from the defensive role into which it was thrust. There is no doubt that a growing theme in domestic politics will continue to be the role of the press. The courts are now deeply into the act with rulings which are not always consistent. Politicians are increasingly finding the press, especially the elite press, an easy whipping boy. All this introduces an increasingly nasty tone into our national dialogue. But I fear that it is going to be part of our lives in the foreseeable future, after Watergate, after Agnew, after Vietnam. The poison is deep into the system and it will be very hard and perhaps impossible to get it out.

Richard Holbrooke is Managing Editor of Foreign Policy.

George E. Reedy, Jr.:

I just have one or two points. First of all, I am quite in agreement with most of Galbraith's paper. I do have one problem with the good man theory. In looking over the history of American politics, it seems to me that even in simpler days, even in days when fellow Americans knew each other, we didn't really always wind up with mental, intellectual, and spiritual giants in the White House. We have had quite a few, if we go over the litany, who did not measure up to the standards of, let's say, St. Francis of Assisi or St. Thomas Aquinas. The real genius of the American system is not that it has always produced giants in the White House but quite the contrary. Gary Wills, in his book, *Nixon Agonistes,* makes a very profound point. What he said is that our system doesn't necessarily produce the best man for the office, but it invariably produces an appropriate man for the office. And at times when the American people are confused, at times when they are disunited, at times when they are uncertain of themselves, we get an appropriate man for the office.

I'm not at all certain that there is any way to attract to Washington the kind of men we really can depend upon to lead this Republic through the extreme difficulties of the modern age, and to lead it in the traditions of freedom that are so important to us. But the real genius of the American system, it seems to me, is that it has enabled us to survive men who were bad. It has enabled us to survive men who did not know what they were doing. It has enabled us to survive situations in which we were confused, and in which our government was confused. I think the problem before us today is not quite so much to find a good man. I always like good men. I hope we do find them. I hope we find many of them. But my own experience in life has led me to meet a few saints as well as foul balls. I am sorry to say there have been more foul balls than saints, and a large group of people that are just middling.

The problem with the White House, as I see it, and the problem with the presidency, as I see it, is that we have to strip away from it that air of sanctity, those layers of courtiers, that monarchical air that has enveloped it, not just in this Administration, but which has been creeping over it with increasing strength for many, many years. And we must once again bring the presidency back to a point where the man who holds the office is no longer going to be that sanctified figure whom nobody criticizes to his face, whatever they may say about him many blocks away, whom nobody really ultimately challenges. This is not going to be a simple matter. But I want to identify it as the central problem of the White House, making the President once again a leader who leads, rather than a king who rules.

On the second point, on the whole question of Mr. Thomson's paper, with which I find myself in total agreement, I was supposed to deliver a critique. I really have no critique of the paper *per se.* It gives me no problems. I think its concepts are sound, and I think they are based upon the realities of the situation. And I think to a great extent they are also based upon the concepts that were placed into the Constitution by the Founding Fathers.

I wish to touch upon one point, however, that seems to me crucial. It's very easy to be for freedom of the press right now. What bothers me about it is that this represents a total change from the atmosphere in the country just a few months ago, when it was almost impossible to attend any meeting which did not lead to a vigorous denunciation of the press. It hasn't been too long since the phrase "nattering nabobs of negativity" brought audiences to their feet yelling and cheering. It wasn't too long ago that there were favorable comments from many sides on a statement by the chairman of the Federal Maritime Commission to the effect that it's good to throw a little fear into the press. It wasn't too long ago that we had commissions bemoaning the fact that ours was an irresponsible press and insisting that we need a free press but also a responsible press. And when the uneasy feeling began to spread over the American people that something was wrong within our government, almost every meeting that I attended was virtually certain to have at least one speaker, and usually four or five, who would say somewhere along the line, "But don't forget, the press needs criticism too." Now, all of a sudden the situation has changed. Everybody wants to be on the side of the free press.

I have a very uneasy feeling that the reasons people are for a free press today are no more valid than the reasons most of them had for being against a free press before the change. What has happened to us is this: there was a battle between one newspaper and the White House, a very, very vigorous battle. And it turned out that the one paper was right and the White House was wrong. And because we had this demonstration that the White House was lying and the press was telling the truth—or, let's try to be as objective about this as we possibly can and say that the White House was wrong and the newspaper was right—all of a sudden everybody wants to be on the side of the winner of that particular battle.

The harder thought, the one that somehow must be pounded through to all Americans, is that we must have a free press, not just when the press is responsible, or not just when the press is right, or not just when the press is doing its duty, whatever that may be. We've got to have a free press because the freedom of the press is inseparable from the freedom of expression. It is really worthwhile to re-read the First Amendment to the Constitution. The Founding Fathers did not say, Congress shall make no law abridging the freedom of the responsible press. They did not say Congress shall make no law abridging the freedom of the truthful press. They did not say, Congress shall make no law abridging the freedom of the press that carries out its obligations. What they said was simply that government shall keep its cotton-pickin' hands off the press. And this is not just because the press is some institution out there that should be sanctified.

I always have trouble with these critiques of the press, these concepts that there is a battle going on and we as citizens should sit back and judge who is right and who is wrong. That's not what's happening. If the press can be held to standards of responsibility—and don't forget, someone has to determine those standards of responsibility—then everybody in this audience can be held to standards of responsibility when they speak. The freedom of the press means that if the press is not free to stand up and say whatever it feels like saying, then you aren't free to stand up and say whatever you want to say. I can be critical of the press. I can be extremely critical of the press, possibly more so than most of you because it has been my first love, since I was five years old. But the one thing that is clear out of all this is that if we come to the conclusion that we're for the press right now only because it happened to be right in a certain fight, we aren't going to feel quite the same way a few months later when the errors, all of the things that happen to human beings, creep in. And we have to go back to the basic point, we are for the free press because we are for our own freedom of expression.

George E. Reedy is Dean, College of Journalism, Marquette University and former White House Press Secretary.

Galbraith:

Mr. Thomson and I have been extremely fortunate in our critics and indeed extremely fortunate in the whole discussion. It seems to me this can be explained by two things. First, that we were essentially right in everything that we've said, so our critics have nothing with which really to disagree. And second, they are critics so richly endowed with their own views that they did not wish to comment on ours. For those passing comments as regards to myself, I accept nearly all of them. Pete Lisagor accused me of hindsight. Good Lord, if we don't exercise hindsight, what *do* we exercise? If we don't learn from the past, how are we to learn? Let me say, however, that there were interesting times in connection with the criticism of the Vietnam war; perhaps we all came to it too late. There were some, I would still insist—perhaps this is a bit self-serving and it's certainly intended to be—who came to the criticism earlier than others. I'm a bit disturbed by the suggestion of some of my colleagues that I'm associated with something called a "good people" theory of government. I was urging what I thought was a sensible policy of government, and that, given the sensible policy, given the avoidance of anything requiring secrecy, an excessive organization, a large military establishment, and above all anything requiring theological dogma, we were likely to get better people than if the policies required those things.

Let me now come to one final and difficult point. Everybody here at the *Pacem in Terris III* convocation, judging from their reactions, has wanted for a long while a more sensible policy with relation to China, and to accept, as previous administrations did not, the existence of that not inconsiderable country. And they have wanted a better policy with reference to the Soviet Union—to give at least a trial to the idea that the Russians are not of the devil, and that negotiations, conversations could be opened up. And they also wanted a policy, as far as one can see, that did not play games between the Chinese and the Soviets and did not seek to exploit differences between them. While I would not defend my colleague Henry Kissinger against certain charges leveled against him by Dave Halberstam, I would point out that working with such improbable material as Richard Nixon, Mr. Kissinger has done the things I just mentioned.

Thomson:

I really have virtually nothing to add to Ambassador Galbraith's eloquent endorsement of the several eloquent endorsements of our two papers. We are deeply grateful. There is a certain symmetry, I should say, to the critiques, at least to the message that they moved on to after they dispensed with our two papers. In general, those whose roots were in government denounced and excoriated the government; those whose roots were in the press denounced and excoriated the press. That's all very well. I think Mr. Lisagor was for the reform of both the government and of the press. Mr. Balk was for the reform of the press. Mr. Cronin was for the reform of the presidency. Mr. Halberstam was for the reform of the press. Mr. Holbrooke for reform of the government. Mr. Reedy was in the middle. He was very good. I liked his message. Let me end my statement with the following five sentences. One, the press is not as good as it looks to us this week. Two, the government is not as bad as it looks to us this week. Three, both desperately need scrutiny and even assistance from all of us. Four, both will continue to need each other. And, five, our country needs the survival of both.

CONCLUDING REMARKS
ON THE
PACEM IN TERRIS III
CONVOCATION

Robert M. Hutchins

We come now to the close of this great convocation. And the question, of course, is what have we learned? Well, I would like to rely on unimpeachable authorities. I quoted one of them to you when we opened: Lincoln's statement, "As I would not be a slave, so I would not be a master." And I will give another one to you now, which really says the same thing in the same way. Thomas Jefferson said, "I tremble for my country when I reflect that God is just."

I was brought up in the days of limited government, but was still surrounded by unlimited vistas of American power. We knew we had that power because we had never tried to exert it. Those were the days of Manifest Destiny, and after we had cleaned up on Spain overnight, we were perfectly convinced of the revealed truth this doctrine purported to impart. The attempt thereafter to realize the vistas opened by Manifest Destiny meant unlimited government, and it meant unlimited exploitation of our people and our resources, and unlimited exploitation of other people and their resources. And the main recurring lesson of this convocation, it seems to me, is that modesty, consideration, justice, are indispensable conditions, not merely of living well, but in a world like this, of living at all.

Can we now still summon up those qualities which I think once were there? Are we prepared for the sacrifices, the creative labor, and the reduction in our arrogance that this kind of world requires? These are the main questions put by this convocation. Have we the willingness to try to put together a world in which everybody, everywhere, has a chance to live a human life? I am encouraged to think so by the dedication you have shown in coming here, day after day, to face the facts, many of them very painful. And I expect even more encouragement as the publications, tapes, and follow-up meetings after this convocation roll across the country and as those who have been here spread what they have learned in their own communities. I think you will agree that this has been an inspiring occasion. It has been made so by the thoughtfulness of the speakers and of the audience. Let us make the most of it.

REFERENCE MATTER

Appendix

PACEM IN TERRIS I
New York City, February 17-20, 1965

Ten years ago the encyclical of Pope John XXIII, *Pacem in Terris*, entered history—in the words of French Monsignor Bernard Lalande—like *"un coup de tonnerre."* Robert M. Hutchins recognized it as "one of the most profound and significant documents of our age," and put the Center's Fellows to work analyzing its implications for a major turn-around in world affairs. Of it, Hutchins said: "It was no accident that John XXIII had emphasized, as did Thomas Aquinas before him, that peace is the work of charity and justice, that peace is not merely the absence of war, that peace is the nature of human life everywhere. *Pacem in Terris* began appropriately with a list of human rights. The Pope said: 'The fundamental principle upon which our present peace depends must be replaced by another.' Thus he consigned nuclear arms, nationalism, colonialism, racism, and non-constitutional regimes to the wastebasket of history. He rejected the devil theory of politics, asserting that 'the same moral law which governs relations between individual human beings serves also to regulate the relations of political communities with each other.' "

Two years later the reverberation from the great moral thunderclap that had sounded from Rome seemed to be dying away. So it was that the Center convened in New York, February 1965, *Pacem in Terris I,* an international convocation dedicated to the proposition that the encyclical John XXIII addressed to all men and all nations should not be forgotten. Its recommendations provided the agenda for a great gathering of world secular and spiritual leaders.

The convocation opened with a plenary session in the hall of the General Assembly at the United Nations. It brought together statesmen, scholars, and other "movers and shakers" from socialist and non-socialist states, among then the Secretary-General of the United Nations; the president of the U.N. General Assembly and two of its former presidents; the Vice President and Chief Justice of the United States, an Associate Justice and four U.S. senators; the Belgian Prime Minister Paul-Henri Spaak; the Italian Deputy Prime Minister, Pietro Nenni; leading public figures from the U.S.S.R., Poland and Yugoslavia; two Justices of the World Court; historian Arnold Toynbee, and theologian Paul Tillich.

Robert M. Hutchins, at the Convocation's outset, told the twenty-five hundred participants: "This is not an ecumenical council assembled to debate religious topics. This is a political meeting. The question is: How can we make peace, not peace through the dreadful mechanisms of terror, but peace, pure, simple and durable? If the principles of *Pacem in Terris* are sound, how can they be carried out in the world as it is? If they are unsound, what principles are sound?"

Secretary-General U Thant observed: "Pope John was no intruder in the dust of the political arena. He knew that hard lines could no longer be drawn between what was happening to the human estate, and what was happening to the human soul . . . . It is not for me, a Buddhist, to speculate on his religious significance, but I believe that later historians will regard him as one of the principal spokesmen and architects for vital change in the twentieth century . . . . Pope John recognized that the age of hiding places had come to an end. For the first time, everyone inside the world enclosure was potentially vulnerable to the failure of even well-intentioned men to move beyond old and inadequate responses and methods."

The then Vice President, Hubert Humphrey, said, "*Pacem in Terris* offers a public philosophy for a nuclear era." The Pope had not written "a Utopian blueprint for world peace, presupposing a sudden change in the nature of man. Rather the encyclical presented a call to action to leaders of nations, presupposing only a gradual change in human institutions . . . the building of a world community."

Norman Cousins, who had served in a private capacity as emissary between Pope John, President John F. Kennedy and Chairman Nikita Khrushchev during the post Cuban missile crisis period, said that "space flights, nuclear energy and all other of modern man's spectacular achievements did not have the impress on history of an eighty-one year-old man dying of cancer, using the Papacy to make not just his own Church but all churches fully relevant and fully alive in the cause of human unity and peace. . . . Human advocacy harnessed to powerful ideas continues to be the prime mover. The peace sought by Pope John need not be unattainable once belief in ideas is put ahead of belief in moving parts."

A great theologian raised the question of whether human nature is capable of creating peace on earth. Paul Tillich observed that man's will being hopelessly ambiguous, one should not address an encyclical to "all men of good will: but to all men, since there is bad in the best and good in the worst." Tillich drew a distinction between hope for a world ruled by peace, justice and love, and hope for a world community capable of avoiding self-destruction. He named several grounds for this kind of hope, including the "community of fear" created by the prospect of nuclear war. This ground, he said, at least makes the conflicting powers conscious that there is such a thing as "mankind with a common destiny."

Psychiatrist Jerome Frank pointed out that while man is both killer and saint, modern war is an elaborate social institution that has to be taught to each generation and can be untaught as well. The problem, thought Frank, is not how to create total peace on earth, but how to make the world safe from man's natural aggressiveness by limiting the scope of his conflicts.

The problem of this duality in man's nature and the avoidance of conflict could best be answered, said Grenville Clark, author of *World Peace Through World Law*, by the limiting of national sovereignty. Nations must assign powers to a world body sufficient to enact and enforce laws binding on all nations. "Such powers," Clark stressed, "can only be described as those of government, i.e., a world government." The need for new forms of world governance, in light of the increasing obsolescence of national sovereignty, was a recurrent theme from the Convocation's beginning to its end.

Ambassador Luis Quintanilla, of Mexico, favored revising the United Nations Charter, enlarging the Security Council, abolishing the veto, weighting Assembly votes to represent populations, and giving the organization a monopoly of nuclear force. The chairman of the Constitution Revision Commission of Japan, Kenzo Takayanagi, reported that his Commission had decided *not* to recommend any change in Japan's famous "pacifist" clause, Article IX of the Constitution, which renounces Japan's sovereign right to wage war and possess armaments.

These views met counterargument from believers in "piecemeal" peacekeeping. World Court Judge Muhammad Zafrulla Khan, of Pakistan, pointed out that only a fully sovereign nation can make a firm treaty, or even cede part of its sovereignty to the authority of world law. His U.S. colleague on the World Court, Philip Jessup, emphasized the coral-like way in which law grows; the fact that much international behavior, such as air routes, mail and weather information is already governed by a network of law, which can and does grow; and that "leg over leg the dog went to Dover."

The Convocation turned to discussion of what was then only barely mentionable: "peaceful coexistence." William Fulbright, chairman of the Senate Foreign Relations Committee, said that national ideology, or a coherent system of values, is a source of great strength and creative energy, but also of "appalling danger," since it tends to impose on others "the tyranny of abstract ideas." He proposed that both the United States and the Soviet Union, in order to make peaceful coexistence less precarious, should subordinate their respective ideologies to "the human requirements of a changing world." The Russians, Yevgenyi Zhukov and N.N. Inozemtsev, both leading Party theoreticians, agreed in part with Fulbright.

The Russians declared that states with different social systems can and must coexist, but only on the basis of sovereign equality and noninterference; there can be no coexistence between "oppressor and oppressed." Inozemtsev said Marxist-Leninist ideology does not advocate the export of revolutions and opposes "the export of counter-revolutions."

"Wars of liberation," Zhukov said, "are legitimate exceptions to the Soviet opposition to war." The "coexistence" discussants found it difficult to agree on anything except Fulbright's plea for mutual tolerance and "the cultivation of a spirit in which nations are more interested in solving problems than in proving theories."

Former Ambassador to the U.S.S.R. and Yugoslavia, George F. Kennan, called for sweeping changes in our European policy, to the point of military disengagement in Germany, and a revision of U.S. assumptions—which provided the *raison d'être* for NATO—about Soviet aggressive intentions.

Abba Eban of Israel declared that after millennia of "national histories, mankind has entered the first era of global history." He proposed that all heads of state devote one week of their working year exclusively to the problems of "the human nation." He set forth an agenda: overpopulation, malnutrition, illiteracy, gross inequality of incomes, and the repair of the physical damage man has done to his planet.

The response to Eban's speech demonstrated that the ecumenical spirit invoked by John XXIII was still alive. It could be said to have been translated into political reality by a Convocation at which, for the first time, leaders of the European Communist bloc mingled openly with their counterparts from the West in informal circumstances where no one was an official delegate bound by his nation's formal view—and where the effort was not aimed at national advantage, or even ultimate agreement, but at greater common understanding.

But even as the delegates gathered in New York, the war in Southeast Asia was escalating, and with it the Cold War tensions between East and West.

PACEM IN TERRIS II
Geneva, Switzerland, May 28-31, 1967

Pacem in Terris I ended with a call from those present for a continuation of the effort. In response, the Center a year later assembled at the Palais des Nations in Geneva advisers from the United Nations, the United States, the Soviet Union, Great Britain, Japan, the United Arab Republic, Poland, France, Cambodia and Mexico to consider the possibilities of another convocation in the light of deteriorating international relations. To them Robert M. Hutchins addressed two primary questions: Could the People's Republic of China be persuaded to attend *Pacem in Terris II*? If not, was there any point in discussing the problems of world order with a fourth of the world's people unrepresented? There was scant optimism about the first, but positive response to the second. Academician N.N. Inozemtsev of the U.S.S.R., observing that in any case the Vietnam conflict would be bound to dominate the next *Pacem in Terris* Convocation, suggested a concentrated effort to bring in Hanoi and thereby initiate a direct American contact that might open the way for peace in Southeast Asia.

The Frenchmen present, Pierre Mendès-France, Premier of France at the time of the defeat at Dien Bien Phu, Ambassador Jean Chauvel, a China expert who had recently returned from Peking via Hanoi, and Xavier Deniau, ranking Gaullist member of the Foreign Affairs Committee of the National Assembly, agreed to arrange with the North Vietnamese representative in Paris to transmit to Hanoi a letter suggesting a meeting with representatives of the Center.

In the meantime, another Center adviser, Ambassador Luis Quintanilla of Mexico, departed for Peking to extend the Center's invitation to participate in *Pacem in Terris II*. After receiving a polite rebuff, he proceeded to Hanoi for a private audience with Ho Chi Minh, who indicated he would receive representatives from the Center to discuss Hanoi's participation. Harry Ashmore, Center president, and the late William Baggs, editor of the Miami *News* and a Center Director, undertook the mission with the full knowledge and cooperation of the U.S. State Department.

In early January, 1967, Ashmore and Baggs had a long private audience with Ho Chi Minh, the last granted to Americans before his death, and transmitted to the State Department what amounted to Hanoi's general proposal for settlement of the conflict. In return, they transmitted to Hanoi, on the Department's behalf, a conciliatory letter intended to open up further exploration at the official level. A hard-line secret communication to Ho from the White House, however, effectively cancelled this informal exchange and later led to public recriminations between the Center emissaries and the State Department.

The fortunes of *Pacem in Terris II* thus were directly and inextricably entangled with the background maneuvering between Washington and Hanoi, and the great powers supporting the two sides. However, Ho Chi Minh kept open the possibility of representation at Geneva until the United States launched a new, heightened offensive against North Vietnam in April, lifting the previous ban on attacks against civilian populations. In the wake of Hanoi's withdrawal, the Soviet Union at the last minute also cancelled its participation.

Thus, in May, 1967, *Pacem in Terris II* convened in Geneva not only without the Chinese, but without representatives of the two Vietnams and the Soviet Union. This, in itself, stood as evidence of the critical increase in Cold War tensions in the wake of the stepped-up U.S. military effort in Southeast Asia. However, representatives of seventy nations, including the two Germanys and other Eastern European countries, were on hand to discuss with renewed urgency the theme, "Beyond Coexistence."

In his opening address U.S. Supreme Court Justice William O. Douglas described the Convocation as "a search for peace—not peace in terms of the absence of hostilities, but peace in the sense of the existence of a rule of law . . . . The idea of coexistence is not enough, for minds geared to it will not be sufficiently imaginative to handle the developing crises. Coexistence is the premise when a nation adopts boundaries, and annexing territory cannot be left to unilateral action or to conspiratorial groups. Tribunals must be designated to adjudicate those claims."

Robert M. Hutchins said that the object of the second Convocation was "not merely to continue the discussion but to direct attention to the immediate practical steps that must be taken if the world is to hold together and humanity is to survive. We are here as citizens of the world and friends of mankind. Peace through the medium of war is too dangerous a game to play. Peace through a common fear is not much safer: it has a transitory, insubstantial character . . . . To aim at the survival of all means to work for justice. The question is, how can it be achieved in a world in which national power is the object of all nations and in which the exercise of that power, in what is mistakenly called the national interest, may be met by a countervailing power, exercised under the influence of a similar mistake?"

The world had lost much ground since *Pacem in Terris I.* The Vietnam war had escalated; and the "Six Day War" in the Middle East coincided with the convocation. In spite of this, Hutchins expressed the hope that it would be possible, under the nongovernmental auspices of the Center, to create an atmosphere of exploration which would be difficult to achieve at an official meeting of governmental representatives.

There was at least one concrete gain in that regard. *Pacem in Terris II* marked the first public discussion between representatives of the two Germanys since the end of World War II. Their participation on a basis of full equality at the Convocation was greeted by the European press with headlines. In his presentation, Dr. Gerald Götting of the German Democratic Republic enumerated several points that would form the basis for normalizing relations between the two Germanys: the signing of a treaty to exclude violence between the two states; acknowledgement of existing frontiers; reduction of armaments by both; participation by both in an atom-free, expansible European zone; establishment of diplomatic relations not only between the two governments themselves, but among each and the other members of the international community. Dr. W.W. Schutz of the Federal Republic of Germany stressed the need for an end to East-West confrontation to be followed by East-West cooperation, and European integrations.

Also, there was a spontaneous grouping of the nations of Southeast Asia, less the two Vietnams, under the leadership of Brigadier General Said Uddin Khan of Pakistan, who had been head of the U.N. peacekeeping mission in Indonesia. There was discussion of a neutralized Southeast Asia, independent of both China and the United States, looking to development under a multilateral aid program channeled through the United Nations. Participants included leaders from Thailand, Cambodia, Laos, Malaysia, Singapore, Indonesia and the Philippines. The Center was asked to arrange a follow-up conference in Southeast Asia. General Khan later visited the countries concerned on the Center's behalf, but reported that no such conference would be practical until the fighting in Vietnam had actually terminated. Thus, five years later, the matter stands as a call for action based upon the agreement in principle summarized by Thailand's Foreign Minister Thanat Khoman: "We live in a period of transition from colonialism to a new order marked by cooperation and partnership. We do not follow Western concepts. The West cannot shape our destiny. What is required today is the cooperation of small nations. This is the true solution to peace among nations."

Pacem in Terris II concentrated on the problem of economic development. The most severe challenge to existing bilateral aid arrangements, and even the efforts of the United Nations and its specialized agencies, came from a Latin American, Dom Helder Camara, Brazilian Archbishop of Olinda and Recife. The Archbishop spoke against Latin American oligarchs and those who keep them in power: "Any economic system that assures prosperity only to a small group precludes victory over 'our internal colonialism, our national slavery.' " He added that it is not enough to "legislate beautiful laws . . . What is needed is moral pressure, democratic but strong, in order to subdue the feeble morals of the rich."

Multinational corporations and cartels also came under Dom Helder's attack: "Private initiative is becoming every day more submerged in international trusts, which are the true masters of the world." Later the Archbishop called for anti-trust legislation "on an international scale."

There was a general agreement on a number of points:

1) The colonial era must come to an end, not only politically but also economically;

2) The developing nations need aid, but this aid should be given multilaterally rather than bilaterally;

3) To this end, a new means of transfer should be set up, as suggested by the *Populorum Progressio* of Pope Paul VI, and reiterated forcefully in a special message from him to the Convocation. The U.N. Special Fund or some other agent might serve, if financed by the members of the United Nations, through a one percent tax on their GNP, as suggested on various occasions by the French, or by savings on military budgets in the wake of arms reductions, as suggested by Pope Paul.

The Convocation again brought into focus the remarkably conservative concept of international law held by the Soviet Union and its allies. This had been demonstrated at *Pacem in Terris I,* where American and European advocates of an expanding, progressive development of transnational jurisprudence as a substitute for the use of force to settle collisions of interest found themselves aligned against an adamant communist defense of the classical, restrictive concept of the inalienable sovereignty of national states, with international relations to be carried out through traditional diplomacy, treaties, and sanctions.

During the course of *Pacem in Terris II,* however, some Eastern European representatives appeared to be moving in a new direction in their view of international law. Manfred Lachs of Poland, a Judge of the World Court, emphasized, more strongly than anyone else, the obsolescence of present international law. He urged its "adaptation to the great changes wrought by the scientific and social revolutions. International law does not address itself to a timeless situation but to a grim and changing reality."

PACEM IN TERRIS III
Washington, D.C., October 8-11, 1973

Pacem in Terris I demonstrated the degree to which a new interdependence among nations had begun to reshape the world and require that the sovereign powers recognize the global character of the most urgent issues confronting them. *Pacem in Terris II* was a sobering reminder of how the old national tensions nevertheless carried over into the new age, with catastrophic results insured unless the nations found the will to pass beyond the narrow, negative limits of mere coexistence. *Pacem in Terris III*, in a departure from the multinational character of the previous convocations, considered these new global requirements in specific terms of their impact on the foreign policy of a single great power, the United States.

If history is measured by generations we are at the end of the era which takes its name from the Cold War. A quarter-century has passed since the grand alliance of the second world war split apart to leave the U.S.A. and the U.S.S.R. confronting each other along the line in Central Europe where their military forces had come together in victory.

On March 12, 1947, Harry S. Truman announced that the United States would assume responsibility for military support of Greek and Turkish régimes deemed to be threatened by covert intervention from neighboring communist countries. The President acted under a formulation of the national interest, holding that "totalitarian regimes imposed on free people, by direct or indirect aggression, undermine the foundations of international peace and hence the security of the United States." Thus emerged the Truman Doctrine, with its proclamation that the choice facing every nation lay between the democratic system exemplified by the United States, and the alternative of "terror and aggression" inherent in the world-wide communist revolution supported by the Soviet Union.

Whether the Doctrine President Truman directed against the Soviet Union was a response in kind, or served to provoke one, there can be no doubt that the interaction between the two great powers has been the dominant force in international relations since the end of World War II.

Implementation of the Truman Doctrine has determined the main directions of the United States foreign policy still in effect, although already in process of modification in the wake of President Nixon's new openings to Moscow and Peking. In February, 1970, in a message to Congress titled "A Strategy for Peace," the President set forth a new Nixon Doctrine: "We will view new commitments in the light of a careful assessment of our national interests and those of other countries, of the specific threats to those interests, and of our capacity to counter those threats at an acceptable risk and cost." Previously he had redefined the national interest in terms that considerably reduced the almost limitless reach of the Truman Doctrine, and employing the new formulation to justify withdrawing United States ground forces from South Vietnam.

The new Doctrine appears to have been accepted by both the U.S.S.R. and the People's Republic of China as a response in kind to the theory of "peaceful coexistence" as propounded, and currently practiced, by both great powers.

It is against this backdrop that a new American foreign policy must emerge if there is to be one. The minimum formulation is a new balance of power which recognizes that the bi-polarity of the Cold War is no longer applicable to the actual grouping of national interests and capabilities. The great power strategists see the new geopolitical shape of the world as pentapolar, with the vast reaches of the third world still treated in practice as hinterlands of the five metropoles of the northern hemisphere—the United States, the U.S.S.R., Western Europe, China, and Japan.

However, there are those who question whether the formulation of foreign policy in the traditional balance-of-power style may be anachronistic. Professor Stanley Hoffmann of Harvard asks: Does the complex world of the more than 130 nations engaged in a bewildering variety of interstate and transnational relations lend itself to the art of diplomacy which insured, if not peace, at least moderation and some stability before and after the French Revolution?

This is the question with which *Pacem in Terris III* began. In the agenda that followed there was no disposition to denigrate the practical necessities of traditional diplomacy. It is difficult, however, to see how any conceivable rearrangement of existing power groupings can be considered other than transient. The nation-state that survives in theory as the basic unit of power politics is undergoing profound modification in practice. As far back as 1961 Henry Kissinger wrote in *The Reporter*:

> Not even the most powerful country is capable by itself of maintaining security or of realizing the aspirations of its people. One of the paradoxes of our day is that more and more nations are coming into being at the precise moment when the nation-state is becoming incapable of dealing with many of its problems and the interdependence of states is ever more obvious.

Put another way, the political forces at work in the world appear to be dominantly nationalist and therefore separatist, but they are countered by an increasingly powerful economic-technological thrust toward supranational forms. We still live in a world fashioned by the instruments of power, but the American experience in Vietnam has raised doubts that the application of these instruments any longer achieves its stated ends. Perhaps the one thing we can be sure of is that the coming era will continue the marked erosion of the basic assumptions of foreign policy planning, forcing adjustments to meet new conditions affecting in fundamental ways the manner in which nations and peoples deal with each other. These were the matters before the house at *Pacem in Terris III*.

Convocation Committee

Chairman, Harold Willens

Vice Chairmen: Henry C. Broady, Charles H. Dyson,
Daniel E. Koshland, Mr. and Mrs. George McAlmon,
Madeleine H. Russell, Albert B. Wells

Allied Products Corporation
Charitable Fund
Dr. and Mrs. Aerol Arnold
Elaine Attias
Mr. and Mrs. Berkley W. Bedell
Mr. and Mrs. Charles Benton
Mr. and Mrs. John Benton
Louise Benton
Mrs. William Benton
E.A. Bergman
The Bydale Foundation
Carlton E. Byrne
John B. Caron
Mr. and Mrs. John Fenlon
Donnelly
Mr. and Mrs. Sydney J. Dunitz
Asher B. Edelman
Raymond Epstein
Mr. and Mrs. Ray Evans
C.R. Evenson Foundation
Mr. and Mrs. Milton Feinerman
The Franklin Foundation
Dr. and Mrs. Charles O. Galvin
Mr. Sheldon M. Gordon
D.S. and R.H. Gottesman
Foundation
Ms. Beth Gould
Mr. Carl M. Gould
Mrs. Joyce Gould
Mrs. Horace Gray
Mr. and Mrs. David Grutman
Mrs. E. Snell Hall
The Hartford Element
Company, Inc.
Mr. and Mrs. George L. Hecker
Uki and Frank Heineman
Ruth and Paul Henning
Dr. and Mrs. E. Craig Heringman

Mr. and Mrs. Harrison W. Hertzberg
Norman Hinerfeld
Mr. and Mrs. Sterling Holloway
Mr. G. Bruce Howard
Mrs. McKibben Lane
Albert A. List Foundation
Mr. and Mrs. George Lord
Mr. and Mrs. Raymond D. Nasher
Frederick M. Nicholas
Mr. and Mrs. Spencer Oettinger
Patterson-Barclay Memorial
Foundation, Inc.
Mr. Miles Pennybacker
Fred and Gertrude Perlberg
Foundation, Inc.
Mr. and Mrs. Gifford Phillips
Phillips-Van Heusen
Foundation, Inc.
Mr. and Mrs. Rudolph S. Rasin
Joyce Reed Rosenberg
Sarah and Matthew Rosenhaus
Peace Foundation, Inc.
Robert and Theodore Rosenson
Mr. and Mrs. Robert F. Rothschild
Mr. and Mrs. Miles Rubin
Mr. and Mrs. Charles Schneider
Herbert M. Singer
Hermon Dunlap Smith
Carl W. Stern
Mrs. Shelby Storck
Latane Temple
Temkin, Ziskin, Kahn and Matzner
United Brands Foundation
Philip and Emma Wain Foundation
Stephen and Claire Weiner
The Williams Foundation
Mr. and Mrs. Sam Winograd
Executive Director, Peter Tagger

Speakers and Participants

HARRY S. ASHMORE, President and Senior Fellow of the Center for the Study of Democratic Institutions.

ALFRED BALK, Editor, *Atlas World Press Review*.

RICHARD J. BARNET, Co-founder and Co-director, Institute for Policy Studies; former official, U.S. Arms Control & Disarmament Agency.

ELISABETH MANN BORGESE, Senior Fellow of the Center for the Study of Democratic Institutions.

GEORGE BROWN, Jr., (D., Calif.) Member, U.S. House of Representatives.

HARRISON BROWN, Professor of Geochemistry, Science and Government, California Institute of Technology.

SEYOM BROWN, Senior Fellow, The Brookings Institution; Adjunct Professor, The Johns Hopkins School of Advanced International Studies.

HERSCHELLE CHALLENOR, Professor of Political Science, Brooklyn College, City University of New York.

FRANK CHURCH, (D., Idaho) U.S. Senator.

CLARK CLIFFORD, former Secretary of Defense.

JOHN COGLEY, Senior Fellow of the Center for the Study of Democratic Institutions; editor, *The Center Magazine*.

JEROME ALAN COHEN, Director, East Asian Legal Studies, Harvard Law School; Chairman, Subcommittee on Chinese Law, American Council of Learned Societies.

RICHARD N. COOPER, Provost, Yale University; former Deputy Assistant Secretary of State for International Monetary Affairs.

THOMAS E. CRONIN, former Visiting Fellow of the Center for the Study of Democratic Institutions.

JOHN PATON DAVIES, former member, China Policy Planning Staff, Department of State.

JAMES H. DOUGLAS, former Deputy Secretary of Defense; member, Board of Directors, Center for the Study of Democratic Institutions.

CHARLES H. DYSON, Chairman, Dyson-Kissner Corporation; member, Board of Directors, Businessmen's Education Fund.

GLORIA EMERSON, Fellow, Institute of Politics, John F. Kennedy School of Government, Harvard University; foreign correspondent, *The New York Times*.

SAM J. ERVIN, Jr., (D., N.C.) U.S. Senator.

RICHARD A. FALK, Milbank Professor of International Law and Practice, Princeton University.

FRANCES FITZGERALD, author, *Fire in the Lake;* recipient, National Book Award.

WILLIAM FOSTER, former Director, U.S. Arms Control & Disarmament Agency; former Deputy Secretary of Defense.

PAULINE FREDERICK, United Nations correspondent for N.B.C. News.

J. WILLIAM FULBRIGHT, (D., Ark.) Chairman, Senate Committee on Foreign Relations.

JOHN KENNETH GALBRAITH, Paul M. Warburg Professor of Economics, Harvard University; former U.S. Ambassador to India.

RICHARD N. GARDNER, Professor of Law and International Organization, Columbia University; former Assistant Secretary of State.

LESLIE H. GELB, National Security Correspondent, Washington Bureau, *The New York Times;* former Director, Policy Planning Staff, Office of the Secretary of Defense.

NORTON GINSBURG, Dean and Senior Fellow of the Center for the Study of Democratic Institutions.

ARNOLD M. GRANT, member, Board of Directors, Center for the Study of Democratic Institutions.

JAMES P. GRANT, President, Overseas Development Council; former Deputy Assistant Secretary of State.

DAVID HALBERSTAM, former foreign correspondent, *The New York Times;* author, *The Best and The Brightest.*

MORTON H. HALPERIN, Senior Fellow, The Brookings Institution; former Deputy Assistant Secretary of Defense.

JOHN LAWRENCE HARGROVE, Director of Studies and Acting Executive Director, American Society of International Law.

THE REVEREND THEODORE M. HESBURGH, C.S.C., President, University of Notre Dame; Chairman, Overseas Development Council.

STANLEY HOFFMANN, Professor of Government, Harvard University.

RICHARD HOLBROOKE, Managing Editor, *Foreign Policy.*

DAVID HOROWITZ, Editorial writer, *Ramparts* magazine.

HUBERT H. HUMPHREY, (D., Minn.) U.S. Senator; former Vice-President of the United States.

ROBERT M. HUTCHINS, Chairman of the Center for the Study of Democratic Institutions; former President, University of Chicago.

HENRY M. JACKSON, (D., Wash.) U.S. Senator.

NEIL JACOBY, Associate of the Center for the Study of Democratic Institutions; Professor of Business Economics and Policy, Graduate School of Management, U.C.L.A.; former Economic Adviser to Presidents Eisenhower and Nixon.

PHILIP C. JESSUP, former Judge, International Court of Justice; former Professor of International Law, Columbia University.

STANLEY KARNOW, Contributing Editor, *The New Republic.*

ALEXANDER KING, Associate of the Center for the Study of Democratic Institutions; Director-General of the Organization for Economic Cooperation and Development, Paris.

HENRY A. KISSINGER, U.S. Secretary of State.

EDWARD M. KORRY, President, United Nations Association; former U.S. Ambassador to Ethiopia and Chile.

EDWARD LAMB, Chairman, Lamb Enterprises; member, Board of Directors, Center for the Study of Democratic Institutions.

GENE R. LaROCQUE, Director, Center for Defense Information; Rear Admiral (Ret.), U.S. Navy.

MORRIS L. LEVINSON, President, Associated Products; member, Board of Directors, Center for the Study of Democratic Institutions.

SOL M. LINOWITZ, Chairman, National Council of the Foreign Policy Association; former U.S. Ambassador to the Organization of American States.

PETER IRVIN LISAGOR, Chief, Washington, D.C. bureau, Chicago *Daily News.*

FRANCES McALLISTER, Member, Board of Trustees, Center for the Study of Democratic Institutions.

EUGENE J. McCARTHY, former U.S. Senator from Minnesota.

GEORGE McGOVERN, (D., S.D.) U.S. Senator; Democratic nominee for President of the United States.

HANS J. MORGENTHAU, Leonard Davis Distinguished Professor of Political Science, City University of New York.

F. BRADFORD MORSE, United Nations Under-Secretary for Political and General Assembly Affairs.

EDMUND S. MUSKIE, (D., Maine) U.S. Senator.

FRED WARNER NEAL, Associate of the Center for the Study of Democratic Institutions; Professor of International Relations and Government at the Claremont Graduate School, Claremont, California.

SENIEL OSTROW, President, Sealy Mattress Company; member, Board of Directors, Center for the Study of Democratic Institutions.

J.R. PARTEN, Vice-Chairman, Board of Directors, Center for the Study of Democratic Institutions.

PETER G. PETERSON, Vice-Chairman, Lehman Brothers; former Secretary of Commerce.

GERARD PIEL, President and publisher, *Scientific American;* recipient, UNESCO Kalinga Prize.

BERNARD RAPOPORT, President, American Income Life Insurance Company; member, Board of Directors, Center for the Study of Democratic Institutions.

GEORGE E. REEDY, Dean and Nieman Professor, College of Journalism, Marquette University; former White House Press Secretary.

EDWIN O. REISCHAUER, Professor of International Relations, Harvard University; former U.S. Ambassador to Japan.

ABRAHAM RIBICOFF, (D., Conn.) U.S. Senator.

LORD RITCHIE-CALDER, Senior Fellow of the Center for the Study of Democratic Institutions.

NELSON ROCKEFELLER, Former Governor of New York; former Assistant Secretary of State.

JONAS SALK, Director, Institute for Biological Studies; Adjunct Professor in Health Sciences, University of California at San Diego.

MARSHALL SHULMAN, Director, Russian Institute, Columbia University.

RONALD STEEL, former U.S. Foreign Service Officer; Visiting Lecturer, Yale University.

ELEANOR B. STEVENSON, member, Board of Directors, Center for the Study of Democratic Institutions.

JEREMY J. STONE, Director, Federation of American Scientists.

WALTER S. SURREY, Adjunct Professor, Fletcher School of Law and Diplomacy, Tufts University.

PAUL M. SWEEZY, former Visiting Professor of Economics, Harvard University; Editor, *Monthly Review.*

KENNETH W. THOMPSON, former Vice-President, Rockefeller Foundation.

JAMES CLAUDE THOMSON, Jr., Curator, Nieman Fellowships for Journalism.

ROBERT W. TUCKER, Professor of Political Science, The Johns Hopkins University.

REXFORD G. TUGWELL, Senior Fellow of the Center for the Study of Democratic Institutions; member of President Roosevelt's "Brains Trust"; former Governor of Puerto Rico.

STANSFIELD TURNER, Vice Admiral, U.S. Navy; President, Naval War College.

SANDER VANOCUR, Director, Communications Project, Duke University; Consultant, Center for the Study of Democratic Institutions.

PAUL C. WARNKE, Chairman, Board of Visitors, Georgetown University School of Foreign Service; former Assistant Secretary for International Security Affairs, Department of Defense.

HARVEY WHEELER, Senior Fellow of the Center for the Study of Democratic Institutions.

JOHN WILKINSON, Senior Fellow of the Center for the Study of Democratic Institutions.

GEORGE F. WILL, Chief, Washington, D.C. Bureau, *National Review.*

HAROLD WILLENS, Chairman, Factory Equipment Corporation; Chairman, Businessmen's Education Fund; member, Board of Directors, Center for the Study of Democratic Institutions.

ALBERT WOHLSTETTER, University Professor of Political Science, University of Chicago.

HERBERT YORK, Professor of Physics, University of California at San Diego; Science Adviser to Presidents Eisenhower and Kennedy.

CHARLES W. YOST, President, National Committee on U.S.-China Relations; former U.S. Ambassador to the United Nations.

About the Editors

Mary Kersey Harvey is editor of *Center Report,* a bi-monthly publication of the Center for the Study of Democratic Institutions. Previously she was an editor and writer for *The Saturday Review* and *McCall's* and director of the McCall Publishing Corporation Editorial Committee. Mrs. Harvey has lived and worked in both Mainland China and the Soviet Union, in the latter country as coordinator of several "Dartmouth" conferences of Soviet and American public figures. She has served as vice-president of a Washington, D.C. public relations firm, as consultant to the magazine division of Carl Byoir Associates, and to the nationally-televised program, "The Advocates."

Fred Warner Neal, a Center Associate and professor of International Relations and Government at the Claremont Graduate School, California, holds degrees in Economics and Political Science and was both a Nieman and Littauer Fellow at Harvard. Following war-time service, Mr. Neal became a consultant on Soviet affairs to the State Department and later chief of its division of Foreign Research on Eastern Europe. In 1950, he was a Fulbright Research Scholar at the *Institut de Sciences Politiques* in Paris and in 1961-1962 a Fulbright professor at the universities of Lyons and Strasbourg. A former correspondent for the *Wall Street Journal,* Mr. Neal has dealt extensively with the Soviet Union and Eastern Europe as a naval officer, diplomat and scholar. His most widely-known books are *Titoism in Action; U.S. Foreign Policy and the Soviet Union* (a Center publication); *Yugoslavia and the New Communism; War, Peace and Germany,* and *The Role of Small States in a Big World.* Mr. Neal has been instrumental in organizing the Center's three *Pacem in Terris* Convocations.

The Convocation in Sound

The *Pacem in Terris III* convocation, the source for these volumes, was recorded on tape from which the Center has edited a series of 28 audio programs. With the added dimension of sound, you can experience the excitement of the convocation almost as if you had been present. You will hear the interplay between speaker and audience—Senator Sam Ervin's distinctive North Carolina drawl—the demonstrators who twice interrupted the speech of Secretary of State Henry Kissinger—the incisive understatements of John Kenneth Galbraith.

The programs can be used in parallel with the printed volumes to great advantage, particularly in classrooms and discussion groups. They include off-the-cuff remarks and other departures from prepared texts that give valuable insights into the personalities and thinking of the remarkable group of men and women who spoke at *Pacem in Terris III*.

The programs in this series vary in length from 23 to 59 minutes and are available on cassettes or open reels at 3¾ ips. Prices range from $8.50 to $12.00. For a brochure describing the series in greater detail, please write to: Audio Programs, The Center, Box 4446, Santa Barbara, California 93103.

DATE DUE

30 505 JOSTEN'S			

49991